The **LIFE** Styles
of Christian Women

The LIFE Styles of Christian Women

DEE BRESTIN

VICTOR BOOKS®

A DIVISION OF SCRIPTURE PRESS PUBLICATIONS INC.
USA CANADA ENGLAND

Scripture quotations in this book are from the
Holy Bible, New International Version, © 1973,
1978, 1984, International Bible Society. Used
by permission of Zondervan Bible Publishers.
Quotations marked KJV are from the *Autho-
rized (King James) Version.* Quotations marked
TLB are taken from *The Living Bible,* © 1971,
Tyndale House Publishers, Wheaton, IL
60189. Used by permission. Quotations
marked NASB are from the *New American Standard Bible,* © the Lockman Foundation 1960,
1962, 1963, 1968, 1971, 1972, 1973, 1975,
1977. Quotations marked PH are from *The New
Testament in Modern English, Revised Edition,* ©
J.B. Phillips, 1958, 1960, 1972, permission of
Macmillan Publishing Co. and Collins
Publishers.

Library of Congress Cataloging-in-Publication Data

Brestin, Dee, 1944–
      The lifestyles of Christian women / Dee
Brestin.
            p.   cm.
      ISBN 0-89693-911-1
      1. Women — Religious life. 2. Women —
Conduct of life. 3. Esther, Queen of Persia.
I. Title.
BV4527.B69 1991
248.8'43 — dc20   91-21846
                                                  CIP

---

  2 3 4 5 6 7 8 9 10 Printing/Year 95 94 93 92

CONTENTS

Letters from Readers
of Dee Brestin's Book: *The Friendships of Women*

You have certainly stimulated my thinking, the mark of a good writer. At times I'm angry, disagreeing violently, at other times smiling and nodding exacting reactions from my husband who insists on a quote.

Addy Mull
Zimbabwe, Africa

Everywhere I went, and with just about everyone I talked to, I found myself sharing some of your thoughts from The Friendships of Women. . . . *Right now I have twelve copies of my own in circulation. I feel you must know me, for you have spoken of me many times in this book. . . . I read thoughts of my own and feelings of my own that I have never heard anyone put into words.*

Viki Presley
Conyers, Georgia

Once I started to read, I could barely put it down. . . . Thank you for expressing feelings that I have felt and wasn't sure I should feel, for helping me understand my own need for friendship, and for seeing the dark side of friendships as well as the good side.

Pat Stevenson
Anderson, Indiana

I have given away a stack of The Friendships of Women. . . . *I want everyone to read it. I believe it to be the clearest and most biblical explanation of what friendships can and should be.*

Suzanne Schultz
Proctorville, Ohio

As a young woman of God, 24, seeking the Kingdom with all my heart, I want to tell you how much your book is touching and inspiring me!

Kari Miyano
Osaka, Japan

I feel as though I already know you after reading The Friendships of Women. *I feel like you understand the relationships that I've been trying to explain to myself and others for fourteen years! My best friend and I agree it's the BEST book about friendship that we've ever read.*

Julie Hines
Defiance, Ohio

ACKNOWLEDGMENTS

I am indebted to the many kind professionals who helped me with research:

Dr. Alvaro Nieves, Professor of Sociology at Wheaton College, and to the student he recommended, *Karen Eckberg,* who diligently combed The Billy Graham Library for research on the lifestyles of Christian women.

Bill Maddox of The Family Research Council who provided me with invaluable leads for research.

Steven Knock of the University of Virginia who sent me his paper on marital stability and satisfaction and provided me with other helpful leads.

Hope Grant of Christianity Today Institute's Research Department who provided me with fascinating statistics.

Dr. Michael Donahue of The Search Institute who sent me information on sexual lifestyles and allowed me an entire evening to interview him.

Everett Worthington of Virginia Commonwealth.

Bryce Christenson of The Rockford Family Institute.

Anne Schaefer of Josh McDowell Ministries.

Rick Bowers of Christian Financial Concepts.

Dianna Keller of Focus on the Family.

Barbara Kim of Holt International Children's Services.

Liz Duckworth of Scripture Press.

The thousands of women who filled out survey forms anonymously, being vulnerably honest for the sake of helping others.

Personal friends who allowed me to interview them, and whose stories appear in this book.

Prayer partners at my church, and at Sonrise Bible Studies, particularly my sister, Sally Frahm, and my friends, Jean Hueser and Shell Ramey.

Friends Sara Andreesen, Jan Hall, Carole Streeter, Mark

Sweeney, Pam Campbell, and Laura Bush, who gave me valuable pre-editorial help, and particularly to Afton Rorvik, my editor and my friend.

Jan Yost, who befriended our daughter Anne and volunteered to teach her to speak English while I conducted research.

Linda Goodrich, for help at home so I can keep working.

My daughter Sally, for her drawing.

My wonderful husband Steve, who prayed with me, read every word I wrote, and continually advised and encouraged me. To my children still at home, Sally and Anne, who, even as children, are willing to be flexible to support their mother in her ministry.

To my mother and father,
Mr. and Mrs. J.R. Brown of San Diego

For the security of knowing you loved each other and us,
and that we'd always be a family;
for music and laughter;
for good books and long talks;
for a sense of wonder in God and His creation;
for the desire to walk in integrity;
for summers in Ephraim and white Christmases in Wisconsin;
for unfailing love, like that of the Lord.

The Wishing Tree

1 The pungent odor of pine and cedar brings back memories of childhood summers and family drives through Peninsula Park, winding through the woods, watching the light filter through the branches, then ending at Wilson's Restaurant for freshly churned Wisconsin ice cream. Beneath the last smooth swallow of ice cream, nestled in the cone's tip, we found a frozen jelly bean—a surprise for the tourists, a cheerful anticipation for us.

Chloe, our Springer Spaniel, hung halfway out the window, silky black ears flapping in the wind, dreaming of deer, raccoon, rabbit. We all hoped for a glimpse of deer, but we knew we'd never miss Peninsula Park's two reliable highlights: Eagle Tower and The Wishing Tree.

Just into the woods, we stopped at Eagle Tower. The car doors flew open and my sisters and I raced ahead of our parents up and around the seven flights of narrow wooden steps to the lookout. With pounding hearts, we surveyed the panorama: a red ball sinking into the bay, flooding the sky with color; sails, bellied-out, gliding home to the safe harbor of Ephraim. The tower was so high, our parents feared one of us might lean a little too far over the railing and suddenly go hurtling over the cliff of Green Bay.

Piling back into the car, my hopes always began to climb as we passed the stretch of green, fragrant cedars because just around the bend, I'd see it: The Wishing Tree. This enormous birch had bent oddly and grown across the road, making a white arch. Legend promised that *if* you made a wish at exactly the right moment while driving underneath the tree, your wish would come true. I held my breath, closed my eyes, and wished with all my childlike faith.

I wished I'd be beautiful, like my older sisters, the homecoming queens. I could imagine peoples' reactions when my wish was granted. They'd stare as I passed, whispering: "That's Dee Dee Brown—have you ever seen anyone so lovely? Her sisters are pretty—but they can't compare to her."

My wish never came true. I was never transformed between The Wishing Tree and Wilson's—so I found comfort in the chocolate ice-cream cone with the jelly bean at the bottom.

During my teenage years I drove my dad's car slowly under The Wishing Tree because my wish list was growing longer. I wanted to marry a wonderful, sexy man who would give me beautiful children and an extravagant house overlooking the Pacific Ocean.

Living on Top of Eagle Tower

I began planning this dream house in earnest when Steve and I were dating as freshmen at Northwestern University. I'd tear a piece of paper from my philosophy notebook and begin drawing floor plans, prodding him for input.

We'd have a loft, perched at the top of the house and extending over the cliff so we'd have the feeling of being lookouts. It'd be like living on top of Eagle Tower—high above the treetops, overlooking a great body of wild water. The wall facing the ocean would be solid glass, no drapes, and the adjacent wall would be a huge stone fireplace. That way, Steve and I could have the fire flickering in the background as we cuddled on the sofa, watching the pounding surf. We disagreed on whether we should have an indoor or an outdoor pool; I wanted to swim under the sun and the stars, Steve wanted to swim all year long. We thought perhaps we could have an indoor pool with a sliding ceiling. I knew I would be so content: baking chocolate chip cookies while the children slept and the waves rolled in.

My dreams shaped my lifestyle, determining how I spent

my days. I concentrated on Steve in college, married him, and we had our first beautiful son. We didn't have our dream house yet; we lived in a little apartment in Indianapolis where Steve was going to medical school. But Steve told me that when he was a surgeon, we'd head for the Pacific and build our house. Meanwhile, in the little free time we had together, we'd roam the Indianapolis furniture stores, imagining what we'd put in our house. On weekdays, cooped up with the baby, I watched soaps or paged through *Better Homes and Gardens.*

Motherhood wasn't quite what I'd imagined. J.R. was colicky and cried for hours at a time. I was glad for any diversion: a trip to the mall, a bridge game with neighbor women, Christmas. But when those diversions ended, my growing emptiness loomed, like an ominous tumor.

Life seemed so repetitive, so meaningless. One afternoon after our baby had finally cried himself to sleep, I sat down to fold a mountain of diapers. As I folded, I thought, *Is this what I've been waiting for? Is my life going to be simply a series of trivial maintenance duties punctuated by an occasional dinner out or a new sofa? I hate this!*

And I decided that somehow it must be Steve's fault. I remember throwing a pan across the room at him and screaming: "You are not meeting my needs!" (I was being incredibly unfair. Not only was Steve going to medical school, but he was also holding down a job to support us.)

Wearily he asked, "What are your needs?"

Stumped, I shouted, "You should be able to figure that out!"

Like Straws upon a River

The fascinating Book of Ecclesiastes is a portrait of a person who is drifting, attempting to find fulfillment outside God because he does not fathom that God has a purpose for his life. Often, he's wearing blinders, and then his vision is limited to life "under the sun." During these times the author of Ecclesiastes tries to find meaning in life with earthly pursuits:

worldly wisdom, parties, the building of a fantastic house and garden, promiscuous sex with concubines. . . . Yet, after each pursuit, he crawls back broken, crying, "Meaningless, meaningless, my life is utterly meaningless!"

For the first twenty-one years of my life, like the author of Ecclesiastes, I hoped the transitory things under the sun would fill the emptiness in me: physical beauty, chocolate, a house on the Pacific Ocean, arts and crafts. I was floating like a straw upon the river, without purpose, being blown first one way and then another by the world's prevailing winds. I lived from day to day, not seeing much in the future, certainly not eternity. My attempts at fulfillment were futile. I remember gathering with women in my apartment complex (none of whom were believers) to, ironically, paint ornate Easter eggs. As I held my completed egg, I felt like crushing it because it suddenly seemed so silly. Were things like this supposed to make life meaningful? My heart despaired.

A Different Dream—A Different Lifestyle

While I struggled with my dreams, my older sister, Sally, was undergoing a change in her dreams, a change in her lifestyle. Having been presented with the claims of Christ, she'd put her trust in Him, and He'd taken the blinders from her eyes, putting eternal dreams in her heart.

As a new believer, Sally read the Bible in the morning and then she prayed, "My day is yours, Lord. Impress on my heart how you want me to spend it."

And God impressed on Sally's heart that she should drive to Indiana, spend a few days with me, and present the claims of Christ. Though it wasn't a convenient time for her, she obeyed.

I eagerly anticipated Sally's visit as a break from the tedium, but I found my sister changed. Though we'd grown up going to church, God had never been a central part of our lives. But now Sally peppered me with questions: "Who did I think Jesus was? Did I understand why Jesus had died on the cross? Did I know that unless I put my trust in what He had done at the cross that I would not be forgiven? Did I know that Jesus wanted me to give Him my whole life?"

I began to eagerly anticipate the *end* of Sally's visit. But to my dismay, it began to snow. A freak October snowstorm paralyzed Indianapolis, and I was snowbound for three more days with my fanatical sister. As the snow piled up outside, Sally persisted with her questions. During those snowy days, the Spirit began to thaw my icy heart.

On the last day of her visit, I determined to ask Sally a question. She was curled up in a chair, knitting a sweater for our son. I set a tray with chamomile tea on a table between our chairs. Instead of making eye contact, I concentrated on the steaming mug between my hands as I curled up too. Finally, trying to sound casual, I asked: "Sally, when Steve is done with his training, we're planning to move West and build the house I've been telling you about. Do you think that if I gave my life to Christ, He would ask me to give that up?"

Sally's dark hair stayed bent over her knitting for the longest time. (She told me later she was imploring God for wisdom.) When she looked up, she had tears in her eyes, and spoke softly: "Dee, I can't tell you what God is going to ask you to do with your life. But I do know that He is a jealous God, and doesn't want any other gods before Him. And it seems that the house has first place in your heart. So I suspect, in your case, the house would have to go."

Because Sally asked me to count the cost, I didn't jump right into Christianity. I didn't want to give my life to Christ until I was convinced He was God. What if it was all a fairy tale? I didn't want to give up the lifestyle I thought might fulfill me for a mere fairy tale!

During the next week I devoured the books my sister had left behind: *Mere Christianity* by C.S. Lewis; *The Cross and The Switchblade* by Dave Wilkerson; and a modern paraphrase of *The New Testament* by J.B. Phillips. And as I read, my heart cried out to God: "Tell me! Are You real? Could this be true?"

As the days passed, I became increasingly convinced that

Jesus was who He claimed to be. Along with that realization came fear. *If Jesus is God,* I thought, *and if heaven and hell are real, then how could I dare to ignore Him?*

So it was the fear of the Lord which led me, on a November morning in 1966, to kneel and surrender my life to Christ. As Solomon wrote, "The fear of the Lord is the beginning of knowledge, but fools despise wisdom and discipline" (Prov. 1:7).

The moment I whispered my prayer, I saw life differently. The Ecclesiastes-like blinders I'd been wearing fell from my eyes, and God put an eternal dream in my heart—not a dream for beauty, or for a fancy house, but a dream for serving the One who made the universe. And along with the blinders, fell a burden from my back, a burden of guilt I hadn't even realized I'd been carrying. I rose from my knees a different woman.

Changes in my lifestyle came slowly. A quarter of a century later, I am still seeing the tentacles of this world's dreams lose their grip as eternal dreams rise to replace them. Pastor Ralph Larson, one of my pastors, explained that this process is like the new sap rising in the spring which forces the stubborn remnants of the old leaves off the trees. As new dreams begin to rise in my heart, the old dreams fade and fall. My first choice now would not be the transitory things of this world (though I'd still accept beauty, or riches!) but the eternal things: the salvation of my loved ones, the growth of our children into dynamic and joyful servants of God, or the use of my gifts in a way that glorifies God. This is what grips my heart and influences my lifestyle.

One of my first eternal hopes was that Steve would put his trust in Christ too. Steve, born of Gentile parents, had been adopted into a loving Jewish home. Though his adoptive parents were not active at a temple, they still hoped their son would embrace the Jewish faith—and a Jewish wife! Steve had done neither, and now began going to a Free Methodist Church with me. (My sister had called a pastor of a large, downtown Free Methodist Church, and he visited us and then steered us to a Free Methodist Church in our own neighborhood.) The people at this church erroneously assumed we were *both* Christians and asked Steve, as a medical student, if he'd be willing to go downtown on a weekly basis and give medical and spiritual help to the homeless. Steve agreed, thinking he could handle the medical and he'd wing the spiritual! During those nights, Steve read the tracts they were giving to those who came for help. "Those tracts put the fear of God in me," he says, "and also told me how to have my fears relieved." Steve put his trust in Christ one cold winter night in Indianapolis' skid row. And God began to put new dreams in his heart.

Yet just as the author of Ecclesiastes vacillated between eternal vision and wearing blinders, Steve and I do too. Steve seems less vulnerable than I because he's always been an extremely disciplined person. For example, he doesn't drink coffee, eat sugar, or watch television because, as he explains simply, "Those things aren't good for me." And he seems puzzled that anyone would do otherwise!

It takes effort for me to swim upstream, and sometimes I lazily float down the river with my shades on, eating chocolate and watching meaningless television. And while I feel free in Christ to do that occasionally, if I overindulge, I taste again that old, stale, and meaningless lifestyle.

So it is my heart's desire to let the new sap rise within me. I find that my eternal dreams are strengthened by the Holy Spirit, by time spent in Scripture, and by being with sisters in Christ who are living a radically different lifestyle than other women in the world. And it is for this reason I am writing this book.

Taking the Pulse of Christian Women

I want to tell you about women I've met as I've been speaking at retreats. My book, *The Friendships of Women*, has given me the opportunity to observe and listen to thousands of Christian women who've put their trust in Christ: from Albuquerque to Washington D.C.; from Boca Raton to Seattle; from

Minneapolis to Austin; in the plains of Kansas and the mountains of Colorado.*

When my missionary friend, Pat Kershaw, saw my speaking schedule, she said:

> Dee, do you realize what an opportunity you have? You can find out all kinds of things about Christian women. I don't know what you want to ask them, but you should be asking them!

And so I passed out survey forms, four different kinds, asking the women at my retreats dozens of questions about their dreams and lifestyles. I asked about sex, money, and how they spent their time. I took questions from surveys of the general female population and asked them of my respondents. For example, *Ladies Home Journal* found that 31 percent of their readers would encourage their ummarried pregnant daughters to have an abortion.[1] How differently, I wondered, would Christian women feel? One discovery led to another and I'd dolly my camera to another angle.

As they handed back their survey forms many women asked: "What are you finding out? Does knowing Christ make a difference in us — in the way we view and live life?" The complete answer to that question will take a book to answer. But yes, I can tell you that Christ definitely makes a different in the lives of the women I surveyed and that difference has been extremely encouraging to me.

----

*When I asked the women at my retreats a question inspired by The Kennedy Evangelism Program, "If you were to die tonight, why would God let you into heaven?" the answers were quite consistent, showing that most understood and believed the Gospel, the central message of the Scriptures. On the basis of their trust in the shed blood of Christ, they were confident their sin had been paid for, and that God would let them into heaven. Though most of the women were in denominations which I would define as evangelical (Baptist, Mennonite, Free Methodist, Evangelical Free), and a few groups were charismatic, there were women at my retreats from every mainline church (Lutheran, Methodist, Presbyterian, Catholic).

A Nebraska woman expressed her eternal vision this way:

> The culture we live in is one of self-gratification. It is not a Christian culture. We are determined not to be swept up by this: to live simply so that we can have the resources and the time to continually inject our lives into ministry. As foster parents, we've seen Christ transform the lives of dozens of the troubled teens who've been in our home.

Women like this evoke in me the twin sisters of guilt and inspiration. Inspiration is the sister I want to favor, and I pray you will too. Stories like this make the sap rise within us and nurture new dreams in our hearts, dreams that overrule the old, transitory dreams. One mother of two from Virginia wrote:

> I help lead a Bible study on Monday nights in the Fairfax County Jail. I'm being obedient to Christ by visiting Him in prison. I leave that jail praising God for the genuine changes in these women — it is *so* exciting.

Many women inspired me with ideas. Consider this simple testimony from a single woman in Minneapolis:

> Journaling is my way of knowing for sure that I met with God during my quiet time. I write down what He's taught me in the passage I've read.

I found many similarities in convictions wherever I went, similarities that cut across denominational lines, particularly when it came to lifestyle issues that are black and white in Scripture. It was the "gray" issues that uncovered controversial opinions. For example, one mother of five from New Mexico wrote:

> Scripture is clear that children are a gift from God and blessed is the man who has his quiver full of them. Yet

how many Christians have their quiver full? (A quiver holds five arrows.) It seems to me most stop after two kids, just like the world.

When Paul dealt with "gray areas" in Romans 14, he told his readers that one man might be persuaded to live one way, and another a different way. And when it came to "disputable matters," Paul wrote: "Each one should be fully convinced in his own mind" (Rom. 14:5). My goal in this book, is not, for example, to persuade every Christian woman to have five children, or to home-school. I do hope to persuade every Christian woman to allow her lifestyle to be shaped, not by the standard of the world, but by the Holy Spirit's leading, realizing His leading will not be identical for all.

I also expect many godly, single Christian women to choose a different path than Kathy Weeks who tells, in the next chapter, of how she didn't kiss her fiancé until her wedding day. Others of you will disagree with my strong cautions to Christian women who have chosen to be involved in multilevel sales. It is my prayer that though we may disagree on these "disputable matters," we can still love and respect each other and allow the Holy Spirit to help us be fully persuaded in our own minds concerning His convictions for us. For those of you who are using the leader's guide and discussing this book in small groups, I would encourage you not to be afraid of differences in gray areas but to remember the importance of expressing those differences in love.

Recently, I had a difference of opinion on the subject of communion with a woman in my Bible study. She said to me, "I do see this differently than you do, Dee, but that difference will never, ever, divide us. I respect and I love you very much." Her words were sincere, so I was able to listen with hearing ears to her thoughts, and to let them be a vehicle for the Holy Spirit.

My goal, for myself, and for my readers, is to live a lifestyle of significant Christianity. The women I surveyed who concerned me the most were those women whom I would describe as "floaters," whose lifestyles were barely discernable from the lifestyles of secular women. One woman, when asked how her lifestyle varied from one who did not know Christ, wrote:

> All I can think of is that our Sundays are different now—filled with church activities. And I don't swear much anymore.

Some of these "floaters" are new Christians, and their perspective may grow as they do. Others seem to have lost the vision and are now conformed to this world. These women vividly demonstrate the danger of not seeking out God's dreams for our lives but allowing, instead, the dreams of the world to become implanted in our hearts.

In addition to surveying Christian women, I have availed myself of the best research comparing the religious to the nonreligious. I found it fascinating, and I think you will too.*

Esther, a Reflection of Us

Woven into this book is the story of Esther, for the winds that she faced are uncannily similar to the winds in our world today. Just as the people of ancient Persia seemed to be obsessed with wealth, sex, and entertainment—so do Americans. When Esther was young, though she was a believer, she succumbed to the pressure, taking part in a beauty contest that involved performance in bed with the king. Later, however, with God's dream in her heart, she turns and swims upstream.

---

*Often this research studied those who attended church, lumping the committed and the uncommitted together. Though this research therefore tends toward ambiguity, it is still interesting. More helpful, but less plentiful, was academic research done of those in conservative churches. I'm keenly aware that my research of women at my retreats has limitations. I tried to cover dozens of areas which really should be covered one by one in graduate thesis studies. Yet I feel I've gotten a pulse reading, one worthy of reflection and further research.

The prevailing winds that blew young Esther down the river are uncannily similar to the winds of our world today—perhaps because Satan doesn't have any new schemes. The lust of the flesh, the lust of the eyes, and the pride of life determined the lifestyle of the king of Persia, who was obsessed with sex, entertainment, and wealth. It was into this world that Esther was drawn. She was swept downstream perhaps because she lacked a dream of sexual purity.

Before we look at Esther, let's look at Christian women today. Are they clinging to a dream of sexual purity before marriage? Are they resisting the prevailing tides of sexual immorality?

*Fundamentalists have more fun. You can't enjoy sex to the
fullest unless you've spent some time in the wilderness, being
repressed.*

Garrison Keillor[1]

Are We Staying Sexually Pure before Marriage?

2 Kathy Weeks has the kind of beauty I wished for under
The Wishing Tree: a porcelain complexion, long auburn
hair, and a model's willowy build and height (5′11″). I'm not
surprised that when Brad spotted her for the first time at
Southwest Baptist University, he chose the chair next to her.

Kathy told me, in a gentle southern accent, of the dream
God gave to her and to Brad: not to kiss until their wedding
day. That dream, however, was preceded by a different dream.
Kathy explained.

> The very first dream God put in my heart was for a
> Christian husband who could provide dynamic spiritual
> leadership. In my Missouri high school, with only fifteen
> students in my class, there weren't many boys to choose
> from! And since I knew I would only date a Christian
> boy, that narrowed it down a lot further. I did date one
> boy, but he wasn't as strong as I hoped for, and I can
> remember thinking that maybe there just weren't going
> to be any men as strong spiritually as I desired.
>
> When I was a freshman at Southwest Baptist Universi-
> ty, I went to a Discipleship Retreat and Brad came in,
> took the chair right next to me, and introduced himself.
> That was a first for me, for I'd always been introduced to
> men through someone else — but that was characteristic
> of Brad's boldness.

Our relationship started as a friendship. In fact it was *so* friendship-oriented, that for months, I wasn't sure where Brad was coming from. And I remember telling the Lord, "Well, Lord, this *is* a wonderful friendship, and if that's all you want it to be, that's fine."

Brad drove me home that summer, and he stayed for a few days before continuing on to his home. One day he took my hand and held it and I thought, *He's holding my hand! That must mean we're dating!*

The next year a revival team came to the SW Baptist's campus. One of the men shared that he'd not kissed his wife until their wedding day. Brad caught the dream. He envisioned what it would be like, on his wedding day, to realize that he was kissing his wife for the first time. Kathy continued:

It was a little awkward for Brad to approach me with this because he wasn't saying I was the one, but he wanted me to know that, because of this dream, this is where the lines would be drawn.

I was stunned when he told me. Though I'd heard about this, still, it had never been presented to me personally. And at first it was a little hard because I wasn't sure Brad was the one for me, and I didn't have as strong a vision of the wedding day as Brad did. Brad is *very* goal-oriented—once he's set a goal, it's a feat accomplished.

But because we didn't get involved physically, our minds were kept clear, and we both had a confidence in our relationship as it progressed. And the more serious we got, the more excited I became about the dream.

Kathy told her roommate, Angie, about the dream and Angie was very supportive. In fact, when Angie began dating she and her boyfriend made the same pact, though they kept it just until engagement.

Kathy and Brad were married on August 13th, 1988. When

Kathy described her wedding day, her enthusiasm brought tears to my eyes.

> I am a pianist, and I've played for so many weddings. I know that even in the best planned weddings, things go wrong, so I kept telling myself that though this would be a wonderful day, things would go wrong, and I shouldn't let that throw me.
>
> But nothing went wrong! *It was perfect. I believe it was God's gracious blessing on our obedience.* It was all we hoped and dreamed it would be—an absolutely marvelous day. We had a wonderful time of worship during the wedding, and then Brad actually kissed me. It sealed the covenant right there—it was the end—and yet, it was the beginning.

I asked Kathy if it was hard for her to adjust to sexual freedom after having been so disciplined. She smiled understandingly and shook her head:

> I expected it to be an adjustment—not only because we hadn't done anything, but also because I am a very modest person. *But I didn't have any difficulty whatsoever* and I know that was a blessing from the Lord. Sometimes I cannot believe the blessing the Lord has given me—in Brad, who is so wonderful, and in our relationship, which is so strong.
>
> And I would tell young girls to seize this dream. They might say to me, "But it was easier for you, because Brad had the idea." That may be true, and I know it will be awkward for them to explain this dream to the guys they date, but too often we neglect talking about the things that are most important to us, and then we regret it.

Are Kathy and Brad unusual among committed Christians? Yes, they are. Yet their numbers are larger than you might expect. Throughout this country, women told me, in their retreat surveys of how they had waited for marriage to enjoy sexual intimacy. I'd like to share just a few of their testimonies with you.

Women Who Waited

Florida:
My fiancé and I wrote a contract, promising each other we would wait until marriage for all sexual intimacy. God helped us to honor that contract.

Minnesota:
I dated many guys through high school and college and waited until I was really serious to kiss anyone — and then I ended up marrying him!

Colorado:
The kids in our youth ministry get bug-eyed when we tell them holding hands was a big decision for us — even after we were engaged. But we took seriously Solomon's warning "Do not arouse or awaken love until it so desires" (Song of Solomon 2:7).

I admire these couples for clinging to the dream of sexual purity. And my admiration grows for those single women who have no marriage partner in sight and yet are determined to remain pure. Here are a few of their testimonies.

Iowa:
The guys at work can hardly believe I'm so pure. It is through God's strength in me that I am. I'm not naive, but I'm innocent.

Washington, D.C.:
God has not given me the gift of singleness, for I yearn for a man to love me completely. But if God never gives me the desire of my heart, and at thirty-seven I am

realizing He may not, *I will be faithful to Him,* continually offering up my longings as a sweet sacrifice to Him.

Reliable studies indicate that in the general population, 73 percent of women have sexual intercourse before marriage.[2] In contrast, when I asked the women at my retreats how many of them had engaged in premarital sex *since they were sure of their salvation,* 26 percent had.*

Many of the women at my retreats had not been sure of their salvation in their late teens and had engaged in premarital sex. Later they repented and changed their lifestyle. Here are a few of their testimonies.

Women Who Repented

Nebraska:
My future husband and I were not Christians when we began dating. We accepted Christ later in our relationship. Once we found that premarital sex was against God's will, I went off the pill and we abstained from intercourse for a year before we were married. Believe me—it was tough! However, our sexual relationship now is very sacred and special to us.

Texas:
I was promiscuous as a teen, and I deeply regret the sins of my youth. Some of the consequences will always be

---

*At early retreats I asked simply, "Have you engaged in premarital sex?" Over half had. At later retreats, I rephrased the question, asking "Since you were sure of your salvation, have you engaged in premarital sex?" The numbers dropped dramatically. This told me that it is important to measure intrinsic factors rather than simply church attendance. For example, Josh McDowell is finding that many kids from conservative churches are sexually active. It's very possible to be in a conservative church and yet not have intrinsic faith, especially in one's youth. When McDowell looked at the intrinsic factor of being born again and committed to the Bible, he found that was the number one barrier to being sexually active.[3]

with me—but not the guilt. His death on the cross is sufficient for my sin. I have a clean slate and am committed to keeping it that way, even if I never marry.

Pennsylvania:
It's by the grace of God that I'm still a virgin because I played with fire in my teens. If I understand men correctly, it's harder for them to stop once they get going, and I asked them to apply the brakes pretty far down the hill. I thank God that He protected me until I matured in Him and had the desire to live purely.

Maturity and Sexual Purity

I made an intriguing discovery by comparing the academic studies of Christian high school kids with the studies of Christian college kids: the percentage of kids who were sexually active does not grow significantly in the college years. The following chart demonstrates this encouraging fact.

YOUTH ENGAGING IN PREMARITAL SEX

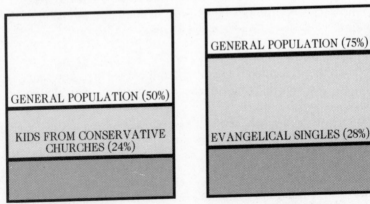

GENERAL POPULATION (50%)

KIDS FROM CONSERVATIVE CHURCHES (24%)

GENERAL POPULATION (75%)

EVANGELICAL SINGLES (28%)

UNDER 18
(Josh McDowell)[4]

OVER 18
(Ferrar and Spilka)[5]

The bad news is that the pressure to become sexually active is beginning at a much younger age. A study cited in *The Wall Street Journal* in 1991 shows that in 1970 only 4.6 percent of 15-year-olds said they had had sexual intercourse, in 1988 that number jumped to 25.6 percent.[6]

Sadly, many kids from Christian homes are not sure of their salvation in their early teens, and many do not have a dream of sexual purity. They are the ones most likely to be swept downstream. In the Song of Solomon we read an interesting passage about one such immature woman:

> We have a young sister,
> and her breasts are not yet grown.
> What shall we do for our sister
> for the day she is spoken for?
> If she is a wall,
> we will build towers of silver on her,
> If she is a door,
> we will enclose her with panels of cedar (8:8-9).

This passage intrigues me because it shows a group of friends combining forces to help protect the young woman in their lives from a world which attacks the dream of sexual purity.

I'd like to share a few stories of mothers who have followed this biblical principle and banded together to "enclose their daughters in panels of cedar" until they become mature and strong:

Nebraska:
When driving to our daughters' volleyball game one night, four of us made a pact. We wouldn't let them rent PG-13 or R-rated movies and watch them in any of our homes.

New Mexico:
We go to a small church. Many of us are not allowing our

children to date before sixteen. Because so many of their peers are in the same boat, our children really haven't complained.

Some of my friends and I have banded together to help our children handle the derogatory influence of contraceptive education in our public school. We've had them sit out of class together, and we've worked individually with them with alternative curricula such as Sex Respect and Teen Aid.

In addition to shielding our young daughters from early dating and impure media influences, I'd like to challenge moms to consider if the Holy Spirit might be leading them to avoid buying Barbie dolls for their daughters. There is no "Thou shalt not buy Barbies" in Scripture, so I simply ask you to weigh my opinion.

Barbie: A Bimbo or a Role Model?

Most of the women at my retreats had bought Barbies for their daughters, granddaughters, or nieces, and many were mystified by my inquiries about Barbie. One woman wrote, in large letters: *Why do you ask about this doll?*

To her, and to others who think I'm choking on a gnat-sized issue, bear with me for a few pages.

To a few discerning secular women, Barbie is not a role model. Susan Reverby, director of the women's studies program at Wellesley College, said: "She's a bimbo. I don't want my daughter to think that being a woman means she has to look like Barbie and date someone like Ken."[7]

But Barbie is viewed positively by millions of little girls. *Forbes* reports, "Nearly half a billion Barbie dolls and members of her family have been sold . . . making Barbie the most popular toy in history. Little girls snap one up every two seconds."[8] A study reported in *Psychology Today* showed that the dolls children play with shape their view of what life is all about. The little girls who played with Barbie placed a high value on her beauty, material assets, and popularity. The researcher, Dianna Foutz, said, "Times have changed since baby dolls and Raggedy Anne. Parents should realize that the media images of dolls often become the ideals of children."[9]

Certainly, many little girls are growing up desiring to be just like Barbie, even many daughters in Christian homes. Many young girls try to become as slim as Barbie and develop eating disorders. Marilyn Motz, associate professor at Ohio's Bowling Green State University, calculated that if Barbie's measurement's were copied to scale, they would be 33-18-28. She says these proportions are "almost not possible anatomically."[10]

But more damaging than wanting Barbie's body is wanting her lifestyle. Barbie, like a female version of the author of Ecclesiastes, spends her days pursuing material things and pleasure. Ken Handler, the son of the founders of Mattel and the namesake for the "Ken" doll, is aware of Barbie's shallowness. He says:

> Barbie should care about more than going to the beach.
> . . . She should care about poverty and suffering in the world. I wish she would work in a soup kitchen, but then she would never sell.[11]

I am sympathetic to the pressure to buy Barbies for little girls. I succumbed to the pressure when our youngest, Anne, kept pleading for a Barbie. (And believe me, there *is* pressure. I smiled when I read the testimonies of mothers of sons in my survey forms. They said that if they *did* have daughters, they would never buy them Barbies. That's how I felt too — before the pressure!) Once I capitulated, one Barbie led to another, and soon our home was overrun with Barbie dolls, Barbie high heels, Barbie fashions, and a Barbie swimming pool. After six months, however, I realized that I had made a mistake. Not only was I concerned because glitzy dates seem like inappropriate play for a six-year-old, but I was concerned that Anne was no longer playing with her baby dolls, no longer dreaming of one day being a mommy. I began to ponder, *What will happen to this generation of little girls? They're not singing lullabies to their babies, or emptying bottles of magically disappearing milk into rosebud mouths, or burping and changing their charges. Instead, they're dreaming of a lifestyle of fashion and glamour, of spending their days at the ski resort, tennis court, and beach.*

And so I bribed Anne (by promising her she could pick out three new baby dolls) into packaging up all her Barbies and putting them in the attic. It was not painless, but Anne has adjusted. She happily plays with her baby dolls now, and I feel that I am helping to put the right dreams in her heart.

Dr. James Dobson has expressed concern that playing with Barbie puts dating dreams into girls' hearts too early. He says that pretending with Ken and Barbie causes our daughters to be interested in dating and sex prematurely. Little girls, he says, "ought to be thinking about more childish things."[12]

A study of 2,400 teens found that 91 percent of those who had begun dating by age twelve had had intercourse by graduation. In sharp contrast, 20 percent of those who waited to date until they were sixteen had had intercourse by graduation.[13] Putting Barbie in the attic was my attempt to stall the dating dream to Anne's heart.

A Minneapolis woman wrote in her survey form that "intercourse was demonstrated to me with Barbie and Ken." And a mother from Kansas wrote: "I regret giving them to my daughters. My oldest daughter, now 31, tells me that they created wrong play and thoughts."

If we can protect our "little sisters in panels of cedar" until they are more mature, they will likely be spared the grief of youthful sexual promiscuity. We should take heart in knowing that many college-age Christians are living purely.

Women Who Try to Repair the Dream Their Way

But what about Christian women who have not managed to live purely? Pastor David Seamands has observed that many Christian women who've engaged in premarital sex feel so ashamed and guilty that they can't seem to receive God's forgiveness.[14] I saw this too. Sorrow tumbled through my survey forms:

Washington:
How I wish I'd been a virgin on my wedding night. It's been twenty years, but my past still haunts our marriage bed.

Nebraska:
My future husband and I got into heavy petting—giving in to premature intimacy seared and demeaned the future things God had planned.

Minnesota:
I'm constantly struggling with thinking I can't have children because God is punishing me for having sex before marriage. I know I'm forgiven—yet that feeling comes back every time I get my period.

I wish this woman, and women who feel as she does, would memorize two passages. First, Luke 1:6-7, where we are told Elizabeth was *blameless* and *barren*. Second, Isaiah 1:18: " 'Come now, let us reason together,' says the Lord. 'Though your sins are like scarlet, they shall be as white as snow.' " God longs for us to trust the power of the blood to make us blameless. Yet even though we are blameless, we may, for reasons we may not understand on this earth, be barren.

David Seamands also noted that many Christian women marry out of guilt. He said, "They reason this way: 'Although we have done wrong, it will be all right if we go ahead and get married.' " Seamands advises, "It's far better to repent now than to regret it later."[15] One woman from Maine gave this bittersweet testimony:

I wish I had waited to marry until I knew who I was, my ministry or call from the Lord. I married my husband at the age of eighteen because I felt obliged and guilty that we'd been sexually intimate. Yet we love each other, plan to stay married for life, and are living proof that God can use any combination for His glory.

Elisabeth Elliot, when asked if a couple who had been intimate should marry, quoted 1 John 1:9 – "If we confess our sins, He is faithful and just and will forgive us our sins and purify us from all unrighteousness." It is far better to admit sin and repent than to try to justify it.

Some women justify their sexual sin by saying they hadn't actually had intercourse. Many women at my retreats wrote statements like this: "We made it! My fiancé and I came very close, but we didn't have intercourse until after the wedding." These women are missing the dream. God wants us to abstain from *all* sexual intimacy until marriage. And because this is such a high goal, and sexual touch is so explosive, Kathy and Brad's very high line makes a lot of sense to me.

Another deception prevalent among Christians is the belief that sexual intimacy is all right if marriage is in the plans. Josh McDowell found that four out of ten (39 percent) kids from conservative churches claimed that if they intended to marry an individual, intercourse with the person would be acceptable.[16] Many of the women at my retreats had slept with their future husbands. When you love someone, and long to sleep with him, it's pretty easy to rationalize that you are married in God's eyes. But you aren't married – that's a deception.

Recently, I discovered a palimony case that I am hoping will awaken young women who are under that deception. Sandra Jennings, who had lived with movie star William Hurt for three years and bore his son, claimed to have a spiritual marriage with him and to be entitled to the rights of a common-law wife. On October 3rd, 1989, The New York Supreme Court rejected those claims and called her a concubine! A concubine in modern America? How fascinating! How unromantic! How like the story of Esther in ancient Persia!

I want to show you, through the William Hurt Trial, how our society has returned to the immoral practice of concubinage. This rising tide of sexual immorality is catching Christians as well.

I learned a great deal about the treachery of tides the year my husband and I lived in Seattle.

A couple should by no means hold hands until betrothed.

Ladies Home Journal (1907)[1]

Sometimes I am just so curious about what a guy will be like in bed, and I want to get the sexual tension behind us, that I sleep with him on the first date. And you know, a lot of people still do it, too. They just talk as if they don't. Face it, everybody always does it sooner than they expect.

Mademoiselle (1990)[2]

How Can Christian Women Resist the Rising Tides?

3 A few years after Steve and I had received Christ, Steve finished medical school. Graduation coincided with the Vietnam war and young doctors signed up with a uniformed service or were drafted. Steve chose The Public Health Service, and we waited prayerfully for our assignment. Imagine our delight when we were assigned to Seattle! Anticipating our move, we placed this ad in *The Seattle Post-Intelligencer:*

> *Responsible* young couple with two little boys, two Springer Spaniels, and a *tight budget* are seeking a rental. We'll take good care of your house!

In response, we received a phone call from a man who said his rental overlooked The Puget Sound. *How*, we wondered, as we drove to the address on Perkins Lane, *could a home in this neighborhood be in our budget?* When we saw the house, we were convinced of a misunderstanding. For there it sat, reminiscent of our relinquished dream house, high on a cliff above the ocean. Ferries and freighters moved on the blue Sound against a backdrop of the Olympic, snow-covered mountains. Surveying the splendid panorama, Steve and I explained again that we were on a tight budget. The man nodded and said softly: "Your ad touched me. I'm an old man and it would give me pleasure for you, your boys, and your dogs to enjoy my house. What can you pay?"

We lived in that house for one year before the Public Health Service transferred us. A few days before we moved, our landlord, Mr. Preston, had a heart attack and died. The gift of that house made us, as new Christians, acutely aware of God's involvement in our lives. It also made us aware of His sense of humor, His graciousness, and His wisdom. He taught us, as I will tell you later, that happiness doesn't come from a house, even a house overlooking the ocean. We also learned an important lesson about the treachery of the tides.

The Treachery of the Rising Tides

In the spring of that year, the boys and the dogs and I would hike down the cliff at low tide to see what we could find.

We wore shoes for the first ten yards because sharp, crusty barnacles covered the beach—barnacles which would rip into my toddlers' tender feet. When we safely reached the sand, we pulled off our shoes and walked barefoot, feeling the wet sand squoosh between our toes. The salty air, the gulls crying overhead, and the gentle lap of the waves awakened us to the joy of life, of creation. The dogs ran and the boys cried with delight as they discovered the life which was uncovered when the moon pulled back the great blanket of the sea: starfish, snail pools, and sand crabs scuttling down in panicked ripples, away from little boys' probing hands.

Once, in our preoccupation with the delights of this world, the tide coming in caught us unaware. So quickly, so stealthily it came. Our three-year-old, J.R., cried out: "Mommy! My shoes!" I turned to see J.R.'s small brown sandals, Johnny's baby shoes, and one of my new tennis shoes bobbing out to sea. Having neglected to place the shoes on a high ledge, I now had to let them go, or risk the lives of my children. I had not taken the kind of precaution a prudent person would have taken, one who was alert to the treachery of the subtly rising tides.

Each year, the tide is a little higher concerning immorality in many areas of lifestyle. Commitments to marriage, to the unborn and the elderly, to sexual purity, to integrity, and to ministering to those who are less fortunate are being washed out to sea by the rising tides. They've come stealthily and caught us unaware. Many Christians have discovered too late that their Nikes are bobbing out to sea with the rest of the world's Nikes.

The first step in resisting the rising tides is recognizing them, seeing corruption and immorality for what they are, no matter how cleverly they are masked, no matter how many of our peers have embraced them.

The story of Esther provides us with a vivid parallel, for the society of Persia into which Esther was drawn was awash in a tide of immorality.

The King of Persia and the King of Porn

King Xerxes, who reigned over Persia, reminds me a great deal of the reigning king of pornography in America: Hugh Hefner. Both men seemed to be given over to the lust of the flesh, as evidenced by their obsession with illicit sex and wine; to the lust of the eyes, as evidenced by their obsession with entertainment that involved pornography; and to the pride of life, as evidenced by their ostentatious display of wealth. Though both "kings" were more decadent than the society in which they lived, their lusts were simply at the crest of a tide sweeping over their countries.

Xerxes hosted a six-month stag party to "display the vast wealth of his kingdom" to Persian military leaders. The description of his palace and grounds reminds me of Hugh Hefner's 5.8 acre Bel Air estate, complete with flamingos, fabulous gardens, and a life-sized robot. Xerxes' estate was said to show, in a blasphemous phrase, "the splendor and glory of his majesty" (Es. 1:4). Likewise, when Hefner surveys his estate, he says, "This is my religion."[3]

One night, when Xerxes was "in high spirits from wine" (Es. 1:10), he called for his beautiful wife, Vashti, to be paraded before the men.

The Targum, an ancient commentary, says that Vashti was asked to appear naked, except for her crown.[4] Josephus confirms this is probable.[5] Whether or not these sources are correct, it is clear that Xerxes' whim was a demeaning one, like asking Vashti to pop out of a cardboard cake. Xerxes did not value women, not even his wife, and so he delivered the humiliating command to Vashti in front of her friends, while she was hosting a private banquet.

It's at this point in the story that we see what a woman may risk if she swims against the flow. Vashti refused to come. (Vashti probably didn't refuse on moral grounds, but for revenge. The Greek historian Herodotus tells of Vashti's character. She was fond of literally burying people alive. In a fit of rage over Xerxes' affair with his brother's wife, Vashti gave the command to mutilate her sister-in-law: to have her nose and ears severed and her tongue torn out!)[6] Vashti found revenge sweet, and I think she enjoyed sending a message back to Xerxes that would deeply embarrass him.

So the lights don't go on, the curtain doesn't go up. And a humiliated Xerxes calls for his counselors who propose that not only should he divorce Vashti (and some commentators say behead), but he should also hold a beauty/sex contest to find a Miss Persia who *will* go with the flow. Dr. John Bronson of Denver says, "I can almost see the king swirling his drink and saying, 'Ahhhh, how delightful. What a marvelous plan!' "[7]

Josephus estimates that about 400 virgins entered the contest.[8] After a year of beauty treatments, each virgin had her night with the king. The one who pleased him the most would be his new wife.

Likewise, Hugh Hefner has an annual contest to elect The Playmate of the Year. In 1989, Hugh surprised everyone by announcing that the latest Playmate of the Year, Kimberly Conrad, had pleased him so much that he was going to marry her. She would be Queen of the Bunny Hutch. In the 20 years since Hugh had moved into the Playboy Mansion, he had had five cohabitants (and one palimony suit), but only Kimberly was to become his wife, ending 36 years of bachelorhood. *People* magazine blazed the news:

> HOLY MATRIMONY! Yes, it's true. Last week Playboy's Hugh Hefner, 63, vowed fidelity to a 26-year old Playmate for Life, Kimberly Conrad. The bride wore white. Hey, she wore *clothes!* Next week: Hell freezes over.[9]

Hefner's marriage was news because it seemed a departure from his playboy philosophy. But though Hefner married Kimberly, and she shortly gave birth to his son, he didn't really elevate her status, for he had her sign an elaborate prenuptial agreement,[10] in an attempt to ensure that she would never be a biblical wife, an equal worthy of honor, a "joint heir." Hugh had not changed to respect women or marriage.

Likewise, the tide in the time of Esther was very demeaning to women. The contest reminds me of a story in *The Arabian Nights.* Every evening King Shehriyar slept with a new bride and then had her executed the next morning. The executions ended when Scheherazade won his heart and became queen.[11]

Xerxes didn't execute the virgins he slept with during the contest for Miss Persia, but if they didn't win, they were demoted to the status of concubines, and very possibly never called for again. They had one night with the king and then, if they were not chosen, became the equivalent of slaves.

Concubines and Cohabitants

Concubinage was a cruel practice, treating women as less than people, using them as objects for sex, childbearing, and housekeeping. When Christ came to earth, He exposed the immorality of concubinage, as well as a myriad of other lifestyle issues. Though concubinage had been practiced since the days of the early patriarchs, Christianity restored the sacred institution of marriage and phased out concubinage.[12] It is as though Christ reached out to women and brought them back to the solid shore. During the nineteen centuries after Christ, if a man lived with a woman sexually, it was almost always because she was his wife, his only wife, his equal, his "fellow heir of the grace of life" (1 Peter 3:7, NASB).

If you look back into history, you can see how long Christ's standard held. Well into the 1900s, most people accepted the standard that intimacy was reserved for marriage. For example, at my retreats, it was very rare for any woman born before 1940 to have engaged in premarital sex. One sixty-five-year-old from Austin wrote: "Why would you ask such a question? That wasn't an option!"

By the 1960s, however, there was a trend toward living together outside of marriage. In 1991 the National Center for Health Statistics found that 50 percent of women between the ages of 25-34 had cohabited.[13]

Though the tide is perilously high, this is a black and white lifestyle issue in Scripture. God's standard remains unchanged. Intimacy outside of marriage is fornication, and God says He will judge fornicators. And a concubine is a concubine, even in the 1990s. I was intrigued to see how a 1983 edition of *Webster's Dictionary* defined concubine: "a woman who cohabits with a man without being legally married to him." This definition is confirmed by our legal system. I made this intriguing discovery recently as a result of miscommunication with my husband.

Often, I don't know what I think until I hear what I say! Therefore I'll meander in conversation, bouncing ideas off those I love. My husband, however, thinks before he speaks. Sometimes he'll forget how I am, and because he is so dear and so goal-oriented, he'll pounce into action long before I'm ready! That happened the day I was expressing my thoughts about my cohabitation research to him. Carelessly, I said, "I wonder if talking to a lawyer who deals in palimony suits would turn up anything interesting..."

And while I was pouring myself a second cup of coffee,

Steve said, "I'll be back in a minute." Then he went to the den and called a lawyer, enlisting her help on my behalf!

Complicated documents began arriving in a steady flow to our mailbox. As the pile on my desk grew, so did our concern about what this request might cost. Our worst fears were realized when a bill for a thousand dollars arrived.

"Please, Lord," I prayed, as I read through the legalese, "help me find *something* worthwhile!" Nothing seemed relevant until I opened the last envelope, the palimony suit against movie star William Hurt.[14] Eureka! The nugget of gold for which I'd been sifting!

William Hurt ("Children of a Lesser God," "Broadcast News," "Accidental Tourist") had lived with Sandra Jennings, a ballerina, for three years before he left her. Because they lived for a time in South Carolina which recognizes common-law marriages, Sandra had hopes of showing that she was, indeed, a "wife" in the eyes of the law.

Sandra moved in with Hurt while he was separated from his wife. Sandra says Hurt promised: "We are going to spend the rest of our lives together." When she became pregnant, he divorced his wife.

According to South Carolina law, Sandra had to prove Hurt's intent. Did he really regard her as a wife, and did others perceive that as his intent? If Sandra could prove this, she might win the $16,000 a month for which she was asking.

The crux of Sandra's case was based on words Hurt spoke to her during a heated argument. Hurt was willing to marry Sandra, but only with a pre-nuptial agreement. Sandra didn't want a pre-nuptial. Sandra went into the bedroom and began to pack. Sandra told the judge that Hurt stormed after her, threw her suitcase on the floor, and said:

> As far as I'm concerned, we are married in the eyes of God. We have a spiritual marriage. . . . We are more married than married people.

Sandra apparently was convinced, for she stayed.

Hurt is not the first man to use the term *spiritual marriage* to try to avoid the real thing. Judge Jacqueline Silbermann gave the following discerning interpretation of Hurt's words:

> The words allegedly spoken do not evince an "intent" to solemnize a marriage but rather the kind of words used by one desiring to continue the parties present state of living together, *i.e.*, in a relationship short of marriage.

Hurt had signed a paternity acknowledgment and Judge Silbermann believed that this demonstrated that Hurt was sincere when he said his commitment to his child was unequivocal. However, Hurt never signed a marriage license, demonstrating a similar commitment to Sandra. Judge Silbermann went on to refer to a decision made in South Carolina generations ago which differentiated between wives and concubines. I could hardly believe my eyes, seeing *concubinage* in a document from 1989. Judge Silbermann quoted the document:

> The difference between marriage and concubinage in the circumstances stated rests in the intent of the cohabiting parties. . . . The intent in marriage consists of living together by agreement by a man and a woman as husband and wife according to what we know to be the law of the land, and according to what we believe to be the law of God. The intent in concubinage consists in a man and woman living together in contrary fashion.[14]

As in the days of Esther, even today, women who live with men outside of marriage are concubines!

There are women who claim to know Christ and also cohabit, but my research shows it is rare.* However, we are being

---

*Only a few women at my retreats had ever cohabited. The only study dealing with cohabitation and churchgoers found that cohabitors were less likely to be churchgoers and more likely to be drug users.[15]

impacted by the tide, for my research shows that approximately a quarter of Christian women sleep with men whom they hope to marry. Sandy Walz who, along with her husband, Bob, is on The Navigator Staff at Kansas State, told me:

> There are Christian college students who are in committed, but not married relationships and are sleeping together. They are dismayed and defensive when Bob and I tell them that what they are doing is not an act of love because it is opposed to God's plan.

These young people have been deceived. They have failed to recognize the tide. They have failed to accept God's standard as the solid shore and so they are being swept out to sea.

It's particularly difficult to resist the tide when your peers are not, particularly your sisters in Christ. I suspect that the main reason Esther capitulated and participated in Xerxes' beauty/sex contest is because the believer to whom she was closest, her guardian, Mordecai, encouraged her to participate. Pastor John Bronson feels that though Mordecai loved Esther, he was politically ambitious.[16] Dr. John Whitcomb points out it was Mordecai who told Esther to hide her Jewish background, which was, he says, "an unthinkable request for a godly Jew."[17] If Mordecai asked her to compete in the beauty/sex contest, it would have been characteristic of Esther to submit, for she had always, we are told, followed Mordecai's instructions when he was bringing her up (Es. 2:20).

Don't Swim Alone

Studies show that women tend to define themselves as part of a web of relationships and therefore have trouble swimming upstream when those around them are floating downstream. One of the secrets to swimming against the flow is to find someone who will swim with you. (Esther eventually discovers this secret, turns, and swims upstream.) As Solomon said: "Though one may be overpowered, two can defend themselves. A cord of three strands is not quickly broken" (Ecc.

4:12). Corroborating this is a study conducted by Dr. J. Timothy Woodroof of 477 freshmen at Christian colleges. He found that the most powerful predictor for sexual behavior was the sexual behavior of that individual's peers.[18] Remember how Kathy Weeks and her roommate Angie gave each other strength with their commitment to sexual purity?

This teaches me, as a mother, the importance of helping my children to develop friendships with strong peers. The time when I have the greatest influence in helping them select their peers is when they are quite young. Prayerfully, I have looked for children from very strong Christian homes, homes that really do not seem to be conformed to this world. Then I call the mothers and tell them why I would like to cultivate a friendship between our children. I have often received support, and we've seen a wonderful, strengthening friendship develop.

Likewise, I have sought out strong Christian friends for myself, and I often ask them to make me accountable in various areas. Through the friendship of one woman, or sometimes a small group of women, I've found strength to swim against my innate tide of laziness and memorize Scripture, pray for others, share my faith, lose weight, go without television, and minister in my community.

If the Tide Is Life-threatening

It is possible that Xerxes and his men would have had Esther beheaded if she didn't submit. It might not have been a simple case of peer pressure.

It could be that a time will come in our lives when we too will be faced with a choice between compromise and death. Will we knuckle under? A secret to swimming against the flow when the pressure is life-threatening is to realize that this life is not all there is. Esther also comes to this point when she makes her famous stand and says, "If I perish, I perish" (Es. 4:16). But as a young believer, Esther didn't have the vision to take this stand, and so she capitulated. She hid her faith for a good three years (and to do so meant eating nonkosher food and probably participating in idol worship), and she did her best in the bedroom competition.

Some commentators exonerate her because she won. But just as I cannot respect Kimberly Hefner for winning the hand of a pornography king through immorality, neither can I respect Esther for winning Xerxes' hand. I *sympathize* and acknowledge that I too have capitulated to pressure, but I believe Esther's capitulation grieved God. She was swept out to sea by the treacherous tides of her times.

In contrast to Esther, young Daniel was able to stand firm when drawn into a pagan society, probably because he had such a strong vision of eternity and of his identity as a believer. Daniel, we are told, "*resolved* not to defile himself with the royal food and wine" (Dan. 1:8). Later, Shadrach, Meshach, and Abednego, who shared Daniel's convictions, were asked to bow down to Nebuchadnezzar's idol. They boldly said:

> If we are thrown into the blazing furnace, the God we serve is able to save us from it, and He will rescue us from your hand, O king. But even if He does not, we want you to know, O king, that we will not serve your gods or worship the image of gold you have set up (3:17-18).

These are the kind of convictions we need to have in order to swim against the flow. And there are Christian women who are doing just that. I believe these women can strengthen us through their lifestyles, as Daniel and his three friends strengthened each other.

Now let me tell you about Christian wives who are committed to making their marriages different than the marriages of secular women. In a society that does not value marriage vows or submission or fidelity, they are swimming against the flow.

I met some of these women when we lived in our Seattle cliff house. It's a good thing I did, for that year in our dream house was the shakiest year of our marriage.

*Respondents who identified themselves as strongly committed
to their religions also reported greater marital
satisfaction. . . . and frequent church attendance is associat-
ed with significantly lower rates of marital disruption.*

*Sociologists D. Jernigan and Steven L. Nock
of The University of Virginia*[1]

Are We Committed to Our Marriages?

4 Though I stopped throwing pans at my husband the day I received Christ, our marriage did not become strong overnight. In Indianapolis, surrounded by a community of believers, I did fairly well swimming upstream. But our move to Seattle separated me from my Christian friends, and suddenly I felt the intensity of the current increase dramatically. Our last years with Indiana Medical School seemed a picnic compared to this internship with the Seattle Public Health Service Hospital!

Steve's hours were merciless. He worked from 7 A.M. until 11 P.M. six days a week, and every third night all night. When he was home, he was asleep. Exhausted and overwhelmed by his job, Steve desperately needed an understanding, supportive wife. Instead, I was an immature Christian, and like the young Esther, I was capitulating to the pressure.

Instead of looking at Steve's needs, I considered only my own. I began to view him as the enemy: someone who had willfully taken me away from friends and family and then abandoned me to two toddlers twenty-four hours a day. *What good,* I thought, *does it do me to be married if my husband is never home?* Once, in anger, I mentioned divorce. Deep down I didn't mean it, and I was having a growing awareness, as a

Christian, of the sanctity of marriage. Yet, in my frustration, I threatened divorce.

Some of my readers may be shocked by this, but it's important to remember that I was a new Christian. My adoption into the family of God has many similarities to our adoption of a five-year-old girl from an orphanage in Korea. Though Anne called us "Om-ma" (Mommy) and "Ab-pa" (Daddy) the day she stepped off the airplane, and her adoption was irrevocable, it took time for her to adjust to an American lifestyle: time to learn the language, to like our strange foods, to overcome her terror of our enthusiastic Springer Spaniel who roamed the house. (Dogs stay outside in Korea.) Anne still struggles with sleeping alone in a bed though it's been over three years.

Likewise, it took time for me to learn to live a godly lifestyle. Concepts such as "submission" and "considering others' needs" were as foreign to me as pizza and English were to Anne.

Also, Steve and I were at a vulnerable time because we did not yet feel a part of a community of believers in Seattle.

Frequent Church Attendance and Marital Stability

A study done by University of Virginia sociologists, Jack Jernigan and Steven Nock, found a positive correlation between church attendance and marital stability.[2] Corroborating this, a study of 3,800 women in Canada found that in 25 years of marriage, of those who go to church, 18 percent divorce; whereas of those who never or rarely go to church 47 percent will divorce.[3] Some researchers believe that conservative churches are more apt to form a community, and provide the watchful eye and encouragement which acts as a barrier to divorce. However, Jernigan and Nock believe that frequent church attenders *in any denomination* will form this community.[4]

While Steve and I were in Indianapolis, believers in our church nurtured us as babes in Christ. Now, pushed out of the nest, between churches, our marriage might have fallen apart except for internal faith. For studies show that internal faith has a positive correlation to marital satisfaction. In my survey forms, for example, I found that the couples who pray often together (only about one third do) are also the most likely to rate their marriages as being "very happy."

Steve, as a new believer in a difficult position, turned to God. His faith caused him to cry out to God, asking Him to help us survive the year.

Internal Faith and Marital Satisfaction

Sociologists Jernigan and Nock reported that whereas church attendance is correlated positively with *marital stability,* it has no effect on *marital satisfaction.* What does impact marital satisfaction positively is internal faith. In other words, going to church may make you less likely to divorce, because of external restraints, but in order to have a satisfying marriage, you need to internalize faith in God.[5] Steve's prayer for our marriage demonstrated his faith.

The first answer to my husband's prayer came through a phone call. Bea, a woman I'd met at a church I had visited, invited me to come to a Bible study and prayer group for young mothers. Because of *my* internal faith, this appealed to me.

On a Thursday morning, I took our toddlers to the church nursery and somewhat fearfully walked upstairs to a room where about ten young women were in earnest discussion around a large table. They stopped when I came in, and I was introduced and quietly took my seat, too shy to participate. When it came time for prayer requests, each woman shared, moving slowly around the table toward me. They were making themselves vulnerable, telling of financial needs, parenting struggles, etc. I wanted prayer for my marriage, my loneliness — but tears prevented me from finishing. I was so embarrassed. I couldn't believe I was crying in front of a group of strangers, but I was, and I couldn't stop.

I'll never forget their response. Clarice, the leader, asked the women to pray for me. (That was going to be tricky, since they didn't know what was the matter!) For the next few minutes, they prayed the best they could, enveloping me with love and support. Suddenly, they didn't seem like strangers anymore.[6]

Several women in that study reached out to me, and through friendship, strengthened me to stand against the pressure during our year of marital instability.

Patti Lynch invited me over for lunch. Though it's been twenty-two years, I can still remember the cloth napkins in silver rings and the layered lemon and lime jello in tall glass parfait dishes. She was saying, with those touches, "I care about you. I'd like to be your friend." She told me, that day, that she'd married a man who had custody of his two daughters. Despite the innate difficulties of being a "step-mom," Christ was enabling them to have a strong marriage.

LaVonne Steiner asked me to be her accountability partner for quiet times. Each day we'd study three chapters in the Bible and then call to briefly share what we'd learned.

And a woman I'll call Kay was a true Titus 2:4 woman. (That passage exhorts older women to instruct younger women to love their husbands.) Though she was only a few years older than I, Kay was much more mature in Christ. She called me and suggested we take a walk with our children around Green Lake because she had a story to tell me. Our preschoolers ran ahead, excited about our outing, giving Kay the privacy she needed to tell me: "I don't think God intended me to marry my husband." I gave Kay a look of surprise, for Rob was a godly man, and they seemed happy together. Kay smiled and explained:

> I had so many doubts when we became engaged that I remember crying out to God for His peace. But you know, Dee, I didn't receive it. I was filled instead with turmoil. And so we called off the wedding. It was then that I received an overwhelming peace.

"But you married him!" I said. Kay nodded as she leaned down to button her baby's sweater against the damp Seattle air.

My parents loved Rob and I have three older unmarried sisters. When I told my mother not to mail the wedding invitations, she went crazy. In response to days of her pleading, I went back to Rob and told him I'd marry him. The peace left me. But I still married him.

The first five years of our marriage were difficult! The only good thing was our sex life. We had waited until marriage and God used that as a balm for our many fights. So many times I thought of bailing out, but God impressed on my heart that even if I had made a mistake and gone against His leading to marry Rob, that He still loved me, *and now, because of our vows, this marriage was His will. I knew with certainty that God was more interested in working through the situation I was in than in having me bail out and start over.* And so I sought God's help like never before.

"How did you do that?" Kay smiled at my question, knowing her words were hitting home.

It's funny the moments I remember. One day Rob agreed to play tennis with me, though he didn't like the sport. He was so bad at it and I remember thinking, "I can't believe I married someone who is so unathletic!" That shows you how immature I was, but I remember praying, "God, help me to love him!"

God answered that prayer in so many ways. I began to attend this women's group, and I learned some practical lessons on being a good wife. A week long Bill Gothard Seminar strengthened me, as did the friendship of women in this church.

Today, ten years and three children later, I can honestly say we have a good, strong, fulfilling marriage.

Scripture's Strong Teaching on Divorce

The tide of divorce is battering at the family structure, and many Christians are falling as well. It isn't hard to find a counselor, even a counselor who calls himself a Christian, who encourages divorce and ignores Scripture's teaching. When a popular Christian author divorced her first husband, she justified it by saying she had made a bad vow and said God doesn't expect His people to keep bad vows. Yet this contradicts the following passage, filled with grave warnings:

> When thou vowest a vow unto God, defer not to pay it: for He hath no pleasure in fools: pay that which thou has vowed. Better it is that thou shouldest not vow, than that thou shouldest vow and not pay. Suffer not thy mouth to cause thy flesh to sin; neither say thou before the angel, that it was an error: wherefore should God be angry at thy voice and destroy the work of thine hands? (Ecc. 5:4-6, KJV)

God seems to permit divorce and remarriage only in the case of adultery (Matt. 19:8-9) and possibly in the case of physical abandonment (1 Cor. 7:15). This hard teaching kept me married to a good man when we were going through stormy, but temporary, circumstances.

Yet when Steve and I were writing a Fisherman Studyguide, *Building Your House on the Lord,* I struggled with God's strong teaching on divorce, for I had a few friends who were in extremely difficult marriages. We needed to send the guide in by the end of the week and the chapter on divorce lay unfinished. I decided, before going to bed one night, that the next day I would finish the chapter on divorce, and somehow, soften the edges.

In the middle of the night I was awakened. I heard a voice within me say, "DON'T TAMPER WITH MY WORD."

The fear of the Lord kept me from doing just that. That doesn't mean that I don't feel compassion for women in unhappy marriages, or unforgiving toward believers who have been divorced (for who hasn't fallen?). It does mean that I desire to put my trust in God's Word and to believe that He cares for us and knows what is best. I have come to appreciate some of the devastating effects of divorce, both through studies, and through the testimonies of friends who have been divorced.

One of my dear friends has openly shared that she was wrong to divorce her first husband, who has since remarried. She says she lives daily with regret for failing to accept God's high standard. She says:

> Holidays are terrible. Finances are complicated. But the worst pain is that I've permanently damaged my children and grandchildren. Sorrow sweeps over me like a wave daily, though it's been twelve years, of the consequences of my selfishness. I tell young women: don't even allow the thought of divorce in your mind. If you do, it's a weed that will grow and grow. God never intended us to leave the man with whom we shared so many firsts: those first struggling years, the births of your children, your first home, Johnny's first steps. . . .

There are Christian women who have divorced for scriptural reasons, and there are some who had no choice: their husbands filed. There are also some who, like my friend, divorced for unscriptural reasons. There is no doubt, however, that commitment to marriage is much higher for Christian women than for secular women. For example, *Ladies Home Journal* asked their readers: "Would you stay in a bad marriage for the sake of the children?"[7] Only one third of those surveyed said they would.

Intrigued, I wondered, how would the women at my retreats respond to that question? I realized that it was a difficult question, and many of the women at my retreats didn't like it. Some crossed out, "for the sake of the children," and wrote, "for the sake of my marriage vows!" Others wrote, "Explain what you mean! Unrepented adultery? There are scriptural grounds for divorce!"

But despite the frustration of the question, it was at least interesting to see that while only one third of the readers surveyed by *Ladies Home Journal* would stick it out, three fourths of the women at my retreats would. Throughout this country, testimony after testimony revealed the strong commitment Christian women have to their marriages. A thirty-year-old from Colorado wrote:

> When I said, before God, "for better or worse, till death do us part," I meant it! My commitment to daily love and support my husband makes me different, I think, from a wife who doesn't know Christ.

Many women gave testimonies similar to this one from a mother of three boys from Nebraska: "I *had* a bad marriage, but because of commitment stayed with it, and God is doing the impossible with my husband and me."

As I began to understand that my marriage vows meant not only staying married, but being a supportive wife, I began to realize that badgering Steve about his hours, over which he had no control, was sinful. When I gave him the support he needed, our marriage changed from a downward to an upward spiral.

After the Public Health Service, we moved to Akron, Ohio where Steve did a four year residency in orthopedic surgery. By this time I was an adolescent, not an infant in the faith, and my marital lifestyle was a testimony to the power of Christ. All around me I saw marriages crumbling, for doctors in training and in the early years of practice have an extremely high rate of divorce. I remember attending a function for residents' wives one night and sitting down at a table where women were venting their emotions about their marriages. One woman, whose marriage later crumbled, said bitterly:

> Some weekend I'm just going to disappear and leave him with the kids. The !@#$%¢& needs a taste of what it's like to have solo round-the-clock care for two babies.

I was shocked that she would talk about her husband like

that in public. And yet I understood! I had been there! *Should I speak up?* I wondered. *Should I tell them how God has changed my attitude and saved my marriage?* Finally, hesitantly, I spoke up and told them, briefly, what had happened to me. It became uncomfortably quiet until someone mercifully changed the subject.

At home that night I realized that I'd tried to put the cart before the horse. It's very difficult to comprehend or desire a Christlike marriage or lifestyle before you know Christ personally. Later, I will tell you about how God helped me and another woman fulfill a dream for reaching those Akron residents' wives. But for now, I want to tell you how He impacted the marriage of one of the women who put her trust in Christ during our time in Akron.

A Story of Christlike Submission

Lee, a petite, winsome brunette, tells a story of her pre-Christian days when her husband was in the Air Force. It is a story that she says demonstrates "my contentiousness as a wife."

> I looked forward to meals with Vince, and it angered me when he was late or hurried—especially if he'd taken time from lunch to jog. One time, when he jogged in late, I marched over to the garbage disposal with his lunch, jammed it down, and said, "If this is how you're going to treat me, fix your own lunch." Then I turned on the grinder.

When Vince and Lee moved to Akron so that Vince could do an internal medicine residency, his hours grew longer. Lee said:

> He'd come home exhausted and hungry, but late, and I'd ruin his meal by telling him that if he really loved me, he would come home to dinner on time. He'd insist he loved me with his whole heart, but the circumstances of

his job kept him away. I resented any authority over me, and I was trying to break him. One day I did. I can still picture him, this big strong Italian, with his head down and the tears flowing.

It was Lee's energy, her vivaciousness, that attracted me to her. She saw me, however, as a religious fanatic. "Remember that book club we were in? You analyzed every book in the light of Jesus Christ. I thought, 'Get real!' "

And yet, God drew us together. "You were kind to me," Lee said, "and you had a strength I lacked. I would go to church, pray to be a good mother, and come home and yell at my kids."

Eventually Lee came to a Bible study I was leading. "There," she said, "I met women who knew God much better than I did, and it stirred a longing in me." Within weeks, Lee put her trust in Christ.

"The Holy Spirit," Lee said, "began to change my rebellious attitude, showing me that my attitude toward authority needed to change." Passages such as 1 Peter 3 and 1 Corinthians 13 convicted her. Lee explained:

> I always needed to have the last word—whether I was right or not. Now God was telling me that it was okay for Vince to be right and that He wanted me to love him unconditionally. That was the beginning of crucifying my contentious spirit. I'd been trying to manipulate Vince by withholding what he wanted—a meal eaten in peace, with a loving wife!

Vince tells about the change he saw in Lee.

> I'd come home late, seven or eight, and expect her to be furious. But she wasn't. She'd reheat supper and sit down with a smile, and a new gentleness. *What*, I wondered, *was going on?* I was genuinely mystified.
>
> One time in church, the Scripture reading was from

Ephesians 5, about wives submitting to their husbands and husbands loving their wives. She looked up at me and smiled. I stooped down and whispered, with amazement, "Is *this* what the difference is?"

Vince's heart was softened. Drawn to the God who had changed his wife, he decided to spend his birthday at a Catholic weekend retreat called "Cursillo." (This is the Catholic counterpart to "Emmaus Walk.") There, on April 19th, 1974, Vince put his trust in Christ. He has celebrated a double birthday ever since.

I recently asked Lee to tell me how Christ is continuing to change their marriage. Reflectively, she said:

> Vince and I are such strong, opposite personalities. We *still* have charged discussions, but at those times, we bring our spirits into obedience to Christ, and the moment passes.
>
> I am acutely aware that I have the power, like the woman described in Proverbs 14:1, to build my house or to tear it down with my own hands. God is helping me to be a wise woman. Because we have the power of the Holy Spirit to temper us, we have a strong, warm marriage.

I believe Lee's story is important because it illustrates the place of submission in creating a strong marriage. However I believe it is important not to stereotype submission as a feminine trait, as something that God expects only of wives.

Scripture *commands* submission for *both* sexes. Christ submitted to God, (1 Peter 2:21-23); and Peter tells us that *in the same way*, wives should be submissive to husbands (1 Peter 3:1); and *in the same way*, husbands should be considerate of their wives (1 Peter 3:7); and *in the same way*, all of us should live in harmony with one another (1 Peter 3:8). Paul also tells believers to be in submission to one another (Eph. 5:21).

If men do not understand that submission is required of

them as well, not only will they miss the blessing of submitting to God, but they may also take advantage of women, whom they feel are called, alone, to submit. I believe this happened in the time of Esther and then history repeated itself in America in the 1970s.

The Backlash in the Time of Esther and in the 1970s

When Vashti refused to be paraded before Xerxes' stag party, the men panicked, saying:

> Queen Vashti has done wrong, not only against the king but also against all the nobles and the peoples of all the provinces of King Xerxes. For the queen's conduct will become known to all the women, and so they will despise their husbands and say, "King Xerxes commanded Queen Vashti to be brought before him, but she would not come." This very day the Persian and Median women of the nobility who have heard about the queen's conduct will respond to all the king's nobles in the same way. There will be no end of disrespect and discord.
>
> Therefore, if it pleases the king, let him issue a royal decree and let it be written in the laws of Persia and Media, which cannot be repealed, that Vashti is never again to enter the presence of King Xerxes. Also let the king give her royal position to someone else who is better than she. Then when the king's edict is proclaimed throughout all his vast realm, all the women will respect their husbands, from the least to the greatest. (Es. 1:16-20).

Pastor John Bronson sums up the above passage like this: "Women, heel! If you don't, we will crush you!"[8]

A strong authoritarian atmosphere often creates unhealthy polarized reactions: rebellion or unquestioning "doormat" submission. Esther, who had a submissive spirit, submitted to things to which God never intended her to submit.

In the early 1970s, the feminist revolution was in high gear. It is characteristic of revolutions to be extreme in the beginning, and many feminists burned their bras and regarded men as the enemy. I believe that in the Christian community there was a panic reaction. Marabel Morgan's *The Total Woman* (1973) suggested women surrender their lives to their husbands, and cater to their quirks, whether it be in "salad, sex, or sports."[9] Meeting your husband at the door in saran wrap was one of Marabel's suggestions. Three million copies were sold and *The New York Times* describes Mrs. Morgan's book as a counterrevolution.*

Many women, like Esther, began to bend over backward to do what they thought was scriptural. They longed for strong marriages, and if this is what God required of them for the fulfillment of that dream, they would do it! One woman told what happened in her small study group, in 1971, when *Fascinating Womanhood* took her church by storm:

> Our fellowship had begun as a Bible study for Christians searching for a New Testament faith. After *Fascinating Womanhood* . . . we were instructed to stifle deliberately the gifts of the Holy Spirit which we had always practiced in church, so that our husbands would be forced to take a more active role. It was constantly emphasized how important the leadership of men was—since Eve had been deceived, our sex was forever unfit for any kind of decision-making or administration.
>
> A friend of mine had a very difficult childbirth with complications. That, she was told, was God's punishment for having been unsubmissive. When her husband recommended she have a tubal ligation, she felt she dare

---

*Marabel Morgan's book has many good suggestions for expressing love. However I believe that during the 70s, in an attempt to swim against the current of the times, that either their philosophies or the reaction to their philosophies resulted in a distortion of the scriptural ideal of the submissive wife.

not disagree. Though tears streamed down her face all the way to the hospital, the operation was performed.

Second Chance, published in 1975, also shows the spirit of the times. David and Sarah Van Wade tell the true story of their divorce, conversion, and remarriage. Their new marital lifestyle was strongly hierarchal. Sarah's submission was a constant issue: she reported every moment of her day and whereabouts to David, even needing permission for lunch with a friend. When he asked her to relinquish her beloved writing career, she sadly obeyed.[11]

Women who were married to men who abused headship, or to unbelievers who had the philosophy of a Xerxes, were particularly vulnerable. Such were the circumstances of a dear friend of mine, whom I will call Jo.

Jo endeared herself to me with her warmth and generosity. When she perceived my stress at having overcommitted myself, she came over and helped me clean. She had a sweet servant spirit, a spirit which her unbelieving husband abused.

After years of infertility, Jo and her husband adopted a son. When Jimmy was beginning school, Jo discovered, to her delight, that she was pregnant. Her husband, however, did not want a baby at this stage in his life. He gave Jo an ultimatum: abortion or divorce. Jo was confused. Should she submit to her husband? Perhaps if she did, she reasoned, God would bring her husband to Himself, or He would stop the abortion in the nick of time. Her husband drove her to the clinic where she had the abortion. No magic hand from heaven swooped down and delivered her. Neither did her husband come to Christ. And, incredibly, during that time, Jo stoically had a baby shower for me!

When Jo came to me, months later, and told me her heartbreaking story, she had begun drinking heavily, joining her husband in his dangerous addiction. Their marital storms escalated into physical abuse. Today, fifteen years later, Jo is divorced, and I am still deeply concerned about her emotional and spiritual well-being. In part, like Esther, she was a victim of a counterrevolution, of a time in which many women lost confidence in their ability to follow God's way without a man's support.

Lest I be misunderstood, I believe in submission and the headship of the husband! And I know how easy it is, because of our sinful nature, to be capricious about submission. But I also believe submission is for women *and* men, and that our first authority is God. There may be times in a woman's life, particularly if she is married to an unbeliever, when she must say, "I love you, and I wish I could do what you are asking, but before God, I cannot."

I believe, on the basis of my survey forms, that Christian America has come back to a healthier scriptural balance.

Christian Marriages in the 1990s

On many survey forms, I asked:

> Which would you say most closely describes your marriage?
> A) ___ Egalitarian (We are co-heirs, mutually submissive)
> B) ___ Hierarchal (My husband is the head of the house and I submit to him unless he delegates an area to me)

Forty percent of the women checked *Egalitarian*, 35 percent checked *Hierarchal*, and another 25 percent checked both answers! One thirty-one-year-old woman from Virginia put it well:

> Only both answers can describe us. We both recognize him as the God-ordained head of the home, but also that we ARE co-heirs. In loving me as Christ loved the church, he does submit to me as well.

And a newspaper editor, also from Virginia, said the same thing, with humor. "We have an egalitarian marriage, but as with *Animal Farm*, he is the more equal pig."

I'm convinced male headship is scriptural, but if it's a constant issue, I believe it's being abused. I like the way Luci Shaw described her marriage to Harold: "Harold is the head of our home, but in twenty-five years, it's only come up twice."

Many women wrote of discovering the Lord's will through prayer and searching the Scriptures with their husbands. If there was an impasse, and a decision needed to be made, their husbands decided. Many testified that their husbands sought to encourage rather than to squelch their gifts.

I heard many testimonies from wives who are desirous of crucifying their sinful nature, and being the submissive wife God longs for them to be. One Kansas wife wrote:

> Every day I dream of being a calm, sweet-spirited wife and mother who makes her home a special place.

An Omaha mother of five explained:

> Ten years ago, I prayed that the Lord would change me into whatever my husband needed in a wife and a woman. Our marriage has not been the same since.

Many today need to take these women's attitudes to heart. For I'm convinced if our attitude is right, and if we are obedient to the Scriptures on marriage, as God intended them to be interpreted, our marriages can be strong and satisfying.

During our last years in Akron, *Redbook* published a survey which demonstrated the impact Christ can have on marital satisfaction. After surveying the sexual lives of 100,000 women, they reported, with shock, that strongly religious wives were the most satisfied sexually! That didn't really surprise me because I'd experienced Christ's power in every area of my marriage. I dashed off a letter in response which *Redbook* published. Men and women in Akron stopped me on the street and praised the letter. I blushed at how I'd revealed myself, but I also felt the pride you feel when the world catches a glimpse of the power of Christ.

Let me tell you the story.

With striking consistency, intensity of feeling about religion parallels the degree of satisfaction women find in the sexual aspect of marriage. "Strongly religious" women are more likely to describe sex as "good" or "very good" than women who are "moderately religious" or "not religious." Women who are "not religious" are significantly more likely to label sex as "poor" or "very poor."

Redbook[1]

Are We Keeping Our Marriage Beds Undefiled?

5 I never imagined that putting my trust in Christ would impact my marriage bed, but it did, and many women give similar testimonies.

The Power of the Blood to Cleanse and Heal

The day I came to Christ, God cleansed me from the guilt I felt over the premarital intimacy I'd known with Steve. Before that momentous day I was a perfect description of Romans 2:15, which says that Gentiles who don't know the law still reveal that they have a law written on their hearts because their consciences, unless they are seared, (as described in Romans 1:18-32) are troubled. Their thoughts vacillate, sometimes accusing, sometimes defending.

Before knowing Christ, I tried to forget about our past — or I tried to justify our actions. Those remedies for sin were ineffective. But when I knelt in our bedroom and placed my trust in Christ's shed blood, grace flooded my heart and I experienced, firsthand, a much better remedy for sin. The removal of my guilt released me to be the responsive wife for which Steve longed.

As I shared earlier, many Christian women struggle to receive forgiveness for sexual sin, but others do indeed allow Jesus to take that burden and free them.

I was particularly encouraged by testimonies from women who'd found healing from childhood sexual abuse. Counseling and the power of God often resulted in a testimony like this from an Iowa mother of four:

> I grew up in a sexually abusive background, but God has set me free to love, in the marriage bed, in the way He intended. He also gave me a beautiful, loving husband.

And one twenty-six-year-old victim wrote, "God healed my hatred for men."

The Power of the Scriptures

I was intrigued by how much counsel Scripture gives concerning the sexual marital relationship. For example, in symbolic language, the author of the Song of Solomon talks of passion, referring to his bride's "garden," which had been locked up before marriage, but now is available to him. He describes his bride's garden as being filled with choice fruits and fragrances (cinnamon, honey, and all the finest spices). He also describes her as a fountain, a well of flowing water. When she asks him to enter the garden, she says she is "faint with love" (Song of Solomon 4–5).

I began to understand that God, who invented sex, longs to bond a husband and a wife through it. He knows that refusing one another can give Satan a foothold. I asked many of the women at my retreats if they applied the following passage to their marriage bed:

> The husband should fulfill his marital duty to his wife, and likewise the wife to her husband. The wife's body does not belong to her alone but also to her husband. In the same way, the husband's body does not belong to him alone but also to his wife. Do not deprive each other except by mutual consent and for a time, so that you

may devote yourselves to prayer. Then come together again so that Satan will not tempt you because of your lack of self-control (1 Cor. 7:3-5).

Ruthie Thune, the senior pastor's wife of a large evangelical church in Omaha, told me that occasionally she or her husband will find a Christian woman who simply refuses her husband sexually after her childbearing years. Ruthie said, "I don't see how she expects to be able to say, 'That's it' and also have a strong marriage—but we are saddened when we see it." However, most of the women who filled out my forms were endeavoring to obey this passage. One happily married forty-year-old woman from Iowa wrote,

> Except for fasting on occasions, I *never* turn my man away. I always encourage him to find a haven in my arms—I belong to him and am at his disposal with no rules or limitations!

More women seemed familiar with the first part of the Corinthians passage (not refusing one another) than the second part (abstaining for prayer). When Steve and I tackled this passage in our study guide, *Building Your House on the Lord,* our editor, Luci Shaw, suspected that abstainers for prayer were rare. It is done however! Pastor Sid Huston of Colorado told me that he "fasts" from sex with his beautiful wife, Karen. Sometimes, he does it for prayer and other times to increase their appetites. He says:

> If we keep on consuming in the area of our appetites and never deny ourselves, we take good gifts, like food and sex for granted. My love and appreciation for Karen has really grown.

The Power of a Passionate and Pure Marriage Bed

Because Steve and I have a treasure to protect, we are committed to keeping our marriage bed undefiled. In part, this means abstaining from entertainment which could leave indelible images on our minds, making us feel that sex is dirty, not God's good plan. One woman wrote, in her survey form:

> I have trouble thinking of the sexual area as beautiful and God-pleasing. I know it is in my heart, but I have trouble applying it.

The lust of the world is very different from the passion of an undefiled marriage bed, but it's easy to be confused, especially if we are carrying baggage from our past. One woman from Washington wrote:

> I didn't make Christ Lord of my life until after I'd seen plenty of raunchy movies. Sometimes, when my husband and I are making love, a movie image will flash in my mind and my passion cools. When that happens, I repeat: "Marriage is honorable in all, and the bed undefiled," (Heb. 13:4a, KJV) and I relax—usually!

Studies show that strongly religious wives are twice as likely to be faithful as nonreligious wives.[2] Less than 6 percent of the women at my retreats had been unfaithful since they were sure of their salvation. Many women wrote that they had been attracted to other men, but that God had given them help in resisting temptation. A thirty-year-old from Colorado wrote:

> The Lord showed me my attraction for another man was really a desire for intimacy—so I began to fill that need in an appropriate way and the attraction subsided. God's grace!

A woman from Minnesota wrote:

> After I was married, I was very tempted by a single man. I physically removed myself from the situation and prayed for God to remove the desire from my heart—and

He did. I am so thankful now.

And a thirty-seven-year-old teacher from Illinois wrote:

> Recently I was attracted to a man (not my husband.) Only my love for God and commitment to my vows kept me from sinning.

That same woman continued her explanation, showing that obedience often pays dividends:

> The longer I am married, the more special the whole concept of being one becomes to me.

Like the above woman, many others mentioned that the spiritual dimension of their marriage had heightened their physical relationship. The two ways of being one seem to interweave, strengthening one another. This, however, can also be a danger area, if God doesn't intend for a relationship to be physical. One woman wrote:

> I would warn Christian women about praying with a man to whom they're not married. It's okay in a mixed group, but not one-on-one. Believe me, I know.

I dealt with the temptations of a lesbian relationship in my book, *The Friendships of Women,* and have received many letters from women who are struggling. Several women wrote that they fell after developing an intense spiritual relationship with another woman. One married woman wrote:

> *Never* would I have dreamt this could've happened to me, but it did. She was my spiritual mentor, and I began to block everyone else out of my life. My dependence shifted from God to her, and it's incredible, but we rationalized our hugs, and then our intimacies. Will I ever feel clean again?

Once Satan gets a foothold, it is an enormous battle to swim upstream. One Colorado woman wrote:

> I have been tremendously attracted to a man other than my husband. I have not acted on my desire. The Navigator Scripture Memory Program has helped me, but Satan has used this [attraction] to keep me preoccupied and unable to fully minister with my life.

I'd encourage this woman and those who identify with her to keep swimming upstream, for I am confident that in time God will give them victory. Those who have given up the fight are filled with regret, like this Florida woman:

> My husband divorced me when he discovered my infidelity. He is trying very hard to forgive me and two years ago, we were remarried. But he can't seem to forget and we are once again separated. I don't know what the future holds for me and our children.

Scripture certainly gives us grave warnings concerning the consequences of adultery. Solomon tells us that men will forgive one who steals much more easily than one who commits adultery. He says, "Whoever does so destroys himself. . . . His shame will never be wiped away" (Prov. 6:32-33).

Be a Bridge to the World

At the Decision School of Writing Karen Mains said that sex may be the closest those who don't know God come to a spiritual experience.[3] They have a hunger for oneness, and according to Solomon, God has also set eternity in their hearts, "yet they cannot fathom what God has done from beginning to end" (Ecc. 3:11). Karen challenged us to use this deep hunger in our society as a bridge to redemption, just as Jesus did with the woman at the well.

I tried to do that when we were living in Akron and *Redbook* came out with their surprising survey. After surveying 100,000 women, *Redbook* found that strongly religious women were the most satisfied sexually. Experts scratched their heads. Weren't religious types supposed to be starched and grim in bed? Yet the survey had been broadly based, carefully done, and conducted without religious bias. The results had to be respected, but the experts were stumped!

I enjoyed seeing the wind knocked out of the stereotype, and I dashed off a letter which *Redbook* published.

> I'm thankful for this survey because it shatters the notion that strongly religious women don't really enjoy sex. In fact, it shows that the reverse is true. I'd like to offer a few points of explanation for this.
>
> A woman who has a close relationship with her God has experienced healing forgiveness for anything in her past. A woman who hasn't drawn near to God may, without realizing it, be carrying guilt. This is bound to affect adversely her sexual relationship.
>
> A woman who has a close relationship with her God has experienced a peace in Him that's going to affect every aspect of her life. A woman who is far from God has an emptiness that cannot be filled with anything but God. She imagines and hopes that other things will fulfill her, but they won't.
>
> A woman who is reading her Bible realizes that God intended that sex within marriage be good and pleasurable. Proverbs 5:18-19 tells a husband to "Rejoice with the wife of thy youth . . . let her breasts satisfy thee at all times, and be thou ravished always with her love."
>
> I, with countless other women, have committed my whole life to Jesus Christ. In return, He has poured out His blessings upon me, in every area of my life. Praise the Lord!
>
> Dee Brestin—Akron, Ohio[4]

One morning, after my letter was published, I was shoveling

my car out of the snow. One of our neighbors walked over to help me. As we shoveled, he said genuinely, "I saw your letter in *Redbook*. Those were intriguing comments!"

I thanked him and plunged my shovel into the snow, glad for a diversion to mitigate my embarrassment. As I shoveled, I felt I should share my story, for my neighbor was asking, in effect, about the hope that was within me (1 Peter 3:15). I told him briefly (perhaps too briefly) about how Christ had changed our lives overnight, but that He continues the process of changing us as we learn more and more of the Scriptures and bring our lifestyles into obedience with them.

Before coming to Christ, my attitude toward married sex had been fairly negative. Ten years later I was extolling its benefits! Likewise, before coming to Christ, my attitude toward motherhood had been one of desperation. I can remember lying down next to our firstborn, who pulled up his legs under his chin and cried constantly with colic, and crying with him. Ten years and two more children later, I was proclaiming motherhood to be one of God's highest callings!

Do you remember when Ann Landers asked her readers how many of them would have children again if they had it to do over? Seventy percent said they wouldn't do it again.[7] How do you think Christian mothers compare?

If I were not a Christian, I would not see mothering as a ministry, a furtherance of God's army. I'd have limited my family size to my plans, and there's a good chance I'd have worked and found providing material possessions for my children more important than being with them.

A twenty-nine-year-old Iowa mother of four

Does Our Lifestyle Demonstrate That We Value Our Children?

6 Ann Landers said that parents of infants wrote to her, mourning the loss of their freedom, describing the confinement, the constant crying, the cost, and their drastically reduced social life. Parents of teens described their children as ungrateful, demanding, and driving them crazy. "Our lives," 70 percent of parents wrote, "would have been better without them."[1]*

While Christian mothers have certainly experienced fatigue and disappointment, they generally have a very different attitude. I asked the women at my retreats: "Would you have children again if you had it to do over?" Less than 1 percent expressed doubt, and for those, it was because they feared for a child's salvation. Most responded like this Florida woman: *"Yes! Yes! Yes! They are the delight of our lives!"*

It didn't surprise me, therefore, to find that Christian couples have more children than non-Christian couples.

Ladies Home Journal found that 28 percent of their readers regretted having children, making me feel Ann's survey was slanted.[2] Yet I find even 28 percent extremely high; these parents are saying, "I wish my children didn't exist!"

We Have More Children

An intriguing report in the *Journal of Demography* found that Protestant women who attend church at least once a month have 2.2 children, whereas those who don't attend have 1.6 children. (The study also reported that except for Hispanics, Protestant women who attend church once a month are now having more children than Catholic women, regardless of their church attendance.[3])

A report in *The Sociological Quarterly* found that couples at the conservative end of religious belief average half a child more than couples at the liberal end.[4] I discovered that the mothers at my retreats average 2.6 children, which is .7 children more than the general population.

It's intriguing to me that Christians have more children, and I believe the reasons for that are numerous. Social data shows that conservative Christians are more likely to marry young,[5] perhaps because of the high value they place on sexual purity and the family. The younger you marry, the more years you have to conceive. In addition, Christian women are less likely to abort unexpected children. However, I believe that there is a more fundamental reason explaining why we have larger families, a reason rooted in our vision and our trust as Christians.

Steve and I sat on our back porch the other night watching our daughters and their friends play "Kick the Can." As their shouts of laughter filled the summer night, we reminisced about how we used to watch our two sons, who are now grown, play this same game. Steve and I have four children, five, if you count our daughter-in-law, Julie, and we do. And we are now in the process of adopting another daughter from a third world orphanage.

That night, as we watched our daughters play, I asked Steve: "How many children do you think we would have had if we had not become Christians?"

"I think," Steve said, reflectively, "that I would have wanted to stop after the boys. Without Christ I would not have seen a purpose for having more, and I would have been afraid to have more." (Please don't misunderstand. I know that God leads in different ways. He has led some couples to make the sacrifice of having no children, or just one, so that they can be free to minister in alternative ways.) It was interesting for me to hear my husband express this view, for I have seen a definite change in his attitude toward children as he has matured in Christ. Years ago when I suggested a third child, he was reluctant. When that third child was ten and I suggested adopting a fourth, he was eager. And recently, Steve suggested adopting a fifth child!

The girls continued their game, making mad dashes toward the can under the darkening cover of night, shrieking with glee. Fireflies lent a magical touch. Cicadas, the huge locusts that thrive in Nebraska, hummed. And I reminisced about how the Lord led us to have these dear girls.

I remember the waves of longing that swept over me as I watched Johnny, our second, climb the bus steps for kindergarten, taking him across Akron to Cuyahoga Falls Christian Academy. He turned as he reached the top step, and waved sweetly. I waved bravely back as J.R., his older brother, hustled him in the door. It squeaked shut behind them.

I leaned against the oak tree and watched the bus disappear around the corner. In the stillness of that September morning, I asked the Lord: "Is this yearning for another child simply an attempt to turn back time and avoid new plans you might have for my time? Am I simply reacting emotionally to Johnny's absence? Or are *You* filling me with this overwhelming desire for another child?"

As fall turned to winter and my desire continued, I approached Steve. He seemed genuinely surprised. He pointed out he'd soon be in a medical practice, and I was beginning to experience success as a writer. "I think we should be content with the beautiful family we have, because we have our hands full with our boys and our ministries."

Though I could see the logic in Steve's reasoning, my desire for a child continued. Lee, my friend whose life and marriage had been transformed by Christ, also had two sons. Then she prayed for a daughter and had Julie. "A daughter," I rhapso-dized to Steve. "Wouldn't it be wonderful if God would give us a daughter?"

Skeptically, Steve raised his eyebrows. But before he left for a convention in Buffalo in the early spring, he kissed me good-bye and said:

> While we're apart, let's each spend some time in earnest prayer about another child. Let's put aside our own de-sires and be a clean slate for God's impressions. Hopeful-ly, when we come together, we'll be like-minded in Christ and we can put this issue to rest.

All week long I prayed, wanting to be open to God's will, yet the desire for a child clung to me. *But what*, I thought, *if Steve's thoughts don't change?* Rarely had we had an impasse since we'd come to Christ—but perhaps one was coming.

The night before Steve returned, I had an idea which I thought might have been prompted by the Holy Spirit. Per-haps we shouldn't use birth control for three months. If I didn't become pregnant, I'd use birth control again, and trust that two children was all God wanted us to have.

When Steve came home, we sat on the sofa and he spoke first:

> I'm still uncertain—but it occurred to me that we're getting better at parenting so perhaps God doesn't want us to stop. How would you feel about not using birth control for three months? But then, if you don't get pregnant, will you trust that God wants us to stay as we are?

In her wedding ring, Billy Graham's daughter, Gigi Tchividjian, and her husband, Stephan, had these words in-scribed, explaining the reason for their marriage: "The same Spirit says the same thing."[6] Now, that Spirit had given Steve and I like-mindedness in Him, and I was confident I'd become pregnant sometime in the spring of 1975. In my prayer journal, I recorded all our requests. We asked God that unless He had a better idea, to give us: a spiritually tender, healthy daughter. I also prayed that she'd have a sunny disposition, that she'd be smart, but not so smart that she'd trust in her mind, that she'd be pretty, but not so pretty that she'd trust in her beauty, that she'd be taller than I am, and that she'd have her daddy's wonderful blue eyes.

But I didn't get pregnant. Stunned to find God's answer was different than I'd expected, I felt a deep sorrow. Yet I also felt we had sought God's will, found it, and that He knew best. Obediently, I went back on birth control. I knew God could override our means of birth control, but in twelve years, He hadn't, and I didn't expect that to happen. Steve felt a sorrow too because by now he really wanted another child. But we both felt that since we'd put out a fleece, we needed to follow through or we would be breaking a vow.

In July of 1975, while I was on birth control, we conceived our spiritually tender, healthy, sunny, blue-eyed daughter. I'll never forget the April morning when Steve laid her in my arms. I had the overwhelming sense that the God who made the universe had been mindful of His unworthy servant.

This was the second time in my life as a believer that I'd relinquished a desire in order to be obedient to God, and He had given it back to me. I know, however, that God does not always give back what we lay before Him.

I looked at our now fifteen-year-old Sally. She and Anne were just yards from me, huddled behind the lilac bush, still playing "Kick-The-Can." Sally peeked out to see if the coast was clear, holding Anne protectively back with one arm. Then she quickly pulled her head back and they giggled conspiratorily. What joy their friendship gave us! How thankful we were for them!

When I first suggested we pray about adoption five years ago, Steve agreed so quickly it took my breath away. We both sensed God's leading, and so we called Holt, a Christian adoption agency.[7] A caseworker, who is now our friend Barb, came and assured us that there were many children in need of a home. The demand is for newborn white American babies, but orphanages in many countries are teeming with children. The most critical need, Barb told us, was for children over five (particularly boys because most people request girls), sibling groups, and handicapped children. These children are categorized as "special needs children." We applied for a special needs child.

About six months later Barb called us and said she felt led to place a healthy five-year-old girl from an orphanage in Seoul with our family. Three months later Anne arrived! She has been such a joy that a few months ago Steve began urging me to consider adopting again. This time, with a full retreat and writing schedule, I was the reluctant one. Yet I am finally beginning to understand that the God who made the universe is smarter than I am, and it's therefore foolish to be closed to His possibilities. I agreed to pray about it with Steve.

One night, while we were praying, Steve had an unusual experience. He looked at me and said, "I just heard a little girl crying out to me."

My feelings, at that point, were a mixture of fear and excitement. I wasn't ready at that point to contact Holt, but just a few weeks later they contacted us. Our caseworker said,

> How would you feel about adopting a girl just a little older than Anne? She's pretty, bright, compassionate — and just has a mild handicap. She's been in a third world orphanage all her life, and she's just been discovered by Holt. She looks like a survivor to me! She's not bitter — in fact, her face radiates joy.

I asked Barb to send all the information they had, including her picture. When it arrived, I walked a few steps from our mailbox and sat down on our grassy hill, unwilling to wait until I got to the house. Her picture fell out — a picture of an endearing child, smiling at me.

When Steve came home, I said, "The information from

Holt has come." He sat down, and, with trembling hands, opened the sheets of background history, the medical report, the social worker's report. He read it all carefully. He stared at her picture. I held my breath as I watched him nod his head.

"Do you want to adopt her?" I asked.

"Yes," he said, confidently. And then added, "But we'll see how the girls feel. And you need to be fully in agreement about this. Otherwise we won't do it."

The girls were positive. I was the one with the most fears. I wrote to our caseworker, telling her I needed some time. I prayed. I sought advice from godly women. My friend Shell wrote us a six page letter, telling us why she thought this seemed right.

Anne and I went out to lunch with my friend Sara Andreesen and her Korean daughter. I am over ten years older than Sara, yet she has been a mentor to me. Her goal is to live on the cutting edge, to cast her bread upon the water, to make a difference in this world. She and her husband Jim have adopted, in addition to their Korean children, a mentally retarded gentleman. Sara also gets up three mornings a week at five to go to a nursing home and help the women bathe and get ready for the day—then she's home before her family is up. She told me, "I know a lot of people would look at what I'm doing and see it as very humbling work—distasteful, perhaps. But I leave that nursing home pumped! To me, this is what life is all about!"

I confessed my fears to Sara that day, as we discussed our possible adoption. My fears particularly centered on this child's handicap. "Sara, Steve has the gift of mercy, but I don't. What kind of mother will I be to her?"

"Do you," she said, "have half a heart to do this?"

"Yes," I said.

"Well then," she said with a smile, "I think you should do it—because half a heart is about all any of us has!"

One by one, women friends encouraged me with prayers and offers of help.

And so, strengthened by my family and my sisters in Christ,

I am stepping out on faith in this adventure. Lord willing, by the time you read this book, this child will be out of the orphanage and in our home.

I am understanding better and better, as I walk this life of faith, what Solomon meant when he said: "The backslider gets bored with himself; the godly man's life is exciting" (Prov. 14:14, TLB). And I am growing in my appreciation, though this is not one of my personal convictions, for the heart of faith that causes some women to be uncomfortable with birth control.

What We Believe about Birth Control

One time, after telling the story of Sally's conception to a group, a woman approached me. She said, "I don't understand how you could perceive going back on birth control as a step of obedience. Birth control is sin."

There are women, both Protestants and Catholics, who agree with this woman. In my survey forms, I asked, "If you have chosen not to use artificial birth control for spiritual reasons, please comment." Some, like this mother of four from Virginia, wrote comments like this:

> My husband and I feel that not only the number but the timing of children should be left up to the Lord, so we've not used birth control.

However most Christian women today, Catholic and Protestants, use birth control and do not feel it is sin. One study found that for church goers individual tastes rather than religious factors underlie reproductive decisions.[8]

As the number of children per family in the general population has decreased, Christians have followed the trend. Shouldn't the number of children for Christians be governed by God's leading rather than personal taste or cultural trends? Only rarely, when I asked the women at my retreats how they determined the size of their families did I get a response like this one, from a Missouri mother of one: "*We'd* like three or

four children, yet we want not our thoughts, but God's will."
I appreciate the thoughtfulness of this Wisconsin mother:

> We don't use the rhythm system because my fertile time
> is my most responsive time, and we agree with John
> MacArthur, who says it violates 1 Corinthians 7:5 (not
> depriving one another). We don't use methods that could
> possibly be an abortifacient, like the I.U.D. or the pill.
> We do use a diaphragm, which acts only as a barrier to
> conception. We believe that children are gifts from God
> and that, if we trust Him, He will provide for each child
> He gives us. So we diligently seek to be open to His
> leading concerning conceiving or adopting.

Christian Women and Abortion

Though most Christian women do not view using birth control as a sin, they feel abortion is sin, that it is the destruction
of a sacred life.

In a 1990 survey *Ladies Home Journal* asked their readers the
following question:

> If your unmarried teenage daughter were to become
> pregnant, which would you be most likely to encourage?
> (A) ___ Abortion
> (B) ___ Adoption
> (C) ___ Raising the child herself
> (D) ___ Raising your grandchild yourself

Thirty-one percent of the *Journal* respondents would encourage their daughter to have an abortion.[9] In sharp contrast
to this sentiment, less than one percent of the women at my
retreats selected abortion as an option for their daughter.
Thirty-four percent of the respondents to the *Journal* had had
an abortion.[10] Seven percent of the women I surveyed had had
abortions since they were saved. This was higher than I expected, and it hurt me to see it. Yet it was still much lower
than the general population. Many of these women had been

young and pressured, like Esther, and now were filled with remorse. One thirty-five-year-old woman wrote: "In a foolish attempt to hide my sin of premarital sex from my parents, I aborted the only child God has ever given me."

Steve and I are emphasizing to our daughters that we long for them to remain sexually pure, but if they fall, we will forgive them. We want them to know that they would have our support in a pregnancy.

Many women who had an abortion or who considered an abortion are now extremely active in the pro-life movement. One mother of three sons wrote:

> Not a day goes by that I don't grieve for the baby I aborted, whom the Lord revealed to me was a girl. I work in a Crisis Pregnancy Center now, and we've had girls live in our home. It's painful, and yet it's also healing to help them give their babies life.

Foster Parenting and Adoption

Many of the women at my retreats enlarged their families through caring for foster children. And though I cannot verify this statistically, I also believe Christians are more likely to adopt children from orphanages overseas. (Since we've adopted Anne, we have met many other couples with a child from another race. Frequently, they're Christians.) My friend, Sara Andreesen, said to me:

> There was a time when Jim and I were discouraged over not conceiving a child. But God *is* faithful. He rerouted us, prepared and flooded our hearts with love for children of another race. For us it didn't seem right to spend thousands of dollars medically to try to get pregnant when the same money brought two beautiful homeless children half-way around the world and made our joy complete.

Another reason our families are larger, I am convinced, is

because applying scriptural parenting principles results in children who are more pleasant to have around!

A Delight in Mothering

Because I came to Christ after becoming a mother, I've tasted the frustration of mothers who've failed to apply scriptural child-raising principles. J.R., our strong-willed firstborn, ruled our home at eighteen months! He'd refuse naps, repeatedly climbing out of his crib. I'd put him back, but he'd climb out again and again until I gave up. Tired and whiney, J.R. was miserable and so was I! I lacked the wisdom, as a new Christian, to see that sticking to boundaries is an act of love.

When J.R. began school at Cuyahoga Christian Academy, his teacher left the room momentarily and he stood on his desk and entertained the other seven-year-olds with jokes. His teacher called us in and said, gently:

> Our goal at this school is to disciple Christian children, not to rehabilitate problem children. Because J.R. does not respect authority, we are going to give him six weeks to learn to do that. I've got some material that may help you to mold his will without breaking his spirit. I hope we'll be able to keep J.R. as a student for he's a lovable, bright charmer—but he needs to learn to respect authority.

Strongly motivated, we devoured the material she'd given us: Dr. Dobson's *Dare To Discipline*[11] and two tapes by Larry Christensen about the right and wrong way to spank.[12] As Steve and I began to practice the scriptural principles in this material, J.R. matured into the kind of son who brings his parents delight. And his teacher saw enough progress to keep him as a student. We'd always loved J.R., but now that he was learning to obey us, we began to think that perhaps we could handle more children!

As we grew in our faith, we also began to catch the vision of raising sons who would be men after God's heart. We began to memorize verses together, have family devotional times, and seize teachable moments. We often acted out Proverbs. One of J.R.'s favorites was: "A wise son brings joy to his father, but a foolish son grief to his mother" (Prov. 10:1). He had many creative ideas, based on experience, for acting out both roles.

The most common dream among the mothers who attended my retreat was for their children to grow into adults who would love the Lord deeply. In hopes of realizing that dream, they were pouring their lives into their children. Here's a sampling of testimonies which I heard repeated again and again throughout this country:

Iowa:
Our five children are our greatest calling from the Lord (and we are not done having children!) We talk of God when we rise up until we go to bed. We don't have a TV. Our four oldest sing at care centers.

Washington, D.C.:
I was discipled by a Campus Crusade Staff person and then discipled a younger girl in college. It's the discipleship idea that enthuses me so about parenting. To do that, I home-school Leigh Ann and Luke, which I see not just as an educational alternative, but as a way of life. We also want our children to know the importance of God's love for ALL peoples and the importance of helping them and sharing the love of Christ with them. Right now, for example, we have a homeless Afghani refugee staying with us.

Nebraska:
More than anything I dream of raising dedicated godly children. I don't want to just preach to our three, but live it, live it, live it!

Because Christian women dream of raising dedicated children, they are also more likely to search for ways to be home with their children instead of working and leaving the care of their children to someone else.

Christian Women Want to Raise Their Children

In a study published by *The Journal of Marriage and the Family*,[13] researchers Mary Morgan and John Scanzoni found that irrespective of denomination, religiously devout women are less likely to continue in the labor force after having children. The researchers seemed to look at this in a negative light, attributing our desire to be homemakers to a rigidity in gender roles. I saw the study in a very positive light—as evidence that Christian women do indeed place high value on the role of a wife and mother, seeing it as their highest calling.

The results of this study intrigued me because frequently other statistical reports, in failing to differentiate between full-time and part-time work, give a misleading picture. For example, one pamphlet shows that 60.5 percent of mothers in the United States are working, while 57 percent of mothers in Rocky Mountain Conservative Baptist churches are working. However, this pamphlet doesn't differentiate between full-time and part-time work.[14]

When I surveyed the mothers at my retreats, 50 percent of them were working, but only 13 percent were working full-time. And among mothers of preschoolers, only 5 percent were working full-time.

Many of the women gave strong testimonies about the importance of staying home with their children.

New Mexico:
I think the main difference between me and a secular mother is that Christ has freed me to feel good about being a stay-at-home mom, showing me that developing character in our son is more important than anything else I could do right now.

Minnesota:
My mom always worked and I hated going to a sitter or

being home alone. The Lord has shown me that staying home is very, very important. I hope never to work full-time. I always want to be there for my children.

Colorado:
When God gave me children, He also called *me* to raise them, to teach them His principles. I've got to be here to do it and I can think of no better way to spend my time during their formative years.

Christian women are also more likely to have support from their husbands to stay home. A study in the *Journal for the Scientific Study of Religion* found not only that religious women are less likely to be in the work force, but also that religious men are more likely to be in the work force.[15] Many women testified to the support their husbands gave them to stay home. One woman from Washington, D.C., who homeschools her children, told the following story:

I gave up a high-paying, "cushy" job with perks galore to stay at home with our daughter. We were in extremely tight financial straits for a while, but God truly honored my husband's and my decision to step out in faith and trust Him. My Jewish neighbor stayed home for two years with her second-born and desperately wanted to remain home longer. But her husband kept mentioning, "We'll fix this," or "We'll remodel that," or "We'll go away on vacation . . . when Ellen goes back to work." Rather than do childcare or tutoring, either or both of which she could have done to earn some money, she went back to work, though her heart yearned to be home. They were not willing to live with less, nor do they have faith in a God who will provide for them.

Parents magazine polled their readers and found that 50 percent of them thought there was no reason a woman shouldn't work outside of the home.[16] In contrast, only 13 percent of the women at my retreats felt that way.

Many of the women who stayed at home with their children found work within the home. When speaking in Iowa, I stayed with Marla Nilson, who provides daycare in her home which resembles an ongoing Vacation Bible School. She's far more than a baby-sitter, she has a vision for making her work count eternally.

Taking in foster children was also mentioned frequently. One woman from Nebraska wrote:

> I didn't have any real interest or aptitude for working with handicapped foster children, but I decided it was something I could do and still stay at home with my children. It's been just enough money to take the edge off my husband's financial anxieties, and the Lord has now really given me a heart for these kids!

Many women who dream of raising strong children are making sacrifices to do it. Many said they were willing to live on one income though it meant a simple lifestyle. Others have given up television. One Kansas mother of four elementary-age boys wrote:

> I want to be so close to God that every word, every step is His. I long to raise godly sons. We are home-schooling and gave up TV five years ago to help with this goal.

Home-schooling appeared so often in my survey forms that it was very clear that this movement has mushroomed in the past few years and is a major part of the lifestyles of many Christian women.

The Home-schoolers

I stayed in Brenda and Ron Bryan's downstairs family room when I gave a retreat in Washington, D.C. The room had been transformed into a sophisticated classroom. Science demonstrations, tapes, books, progress reports, and an elaborate, full-wall history chart set the earnest academic atmosphere. All this is used for one little girl: five-year-old Aimee Bryan. Brenda is using the "Konos" (from the Greek word for cone) curriculum, one of many excellent curriculums available to homeschoolers. Right now Aimee is studying the ear, which is in a unit on the character trait "Attentiveness." Brenda said:

> Another home-schooler and I set up a demonstration of the workings of the ear with chairs, blankets, a hammer, a stirrup, a seashell, etc. Then the three children took turns being the different parts, including crawling through the set-up as sound waves. From there "Konos" branched out into history. We're reading *Helen Keller*, and we watched "The Miracle Worker." We took our Friday field trip to the Gallaudet University for The Deaf. And we studied about people who've been attentive to God's call, like Samuel.

Brenda told me she had resisted home-schooling in the past because she pictured home-schooling moms as being out of the mainstream of life, as "birdseed-eating vegetarians who nursed their children until they were five and taught their sons to crochet." Three years ago only four families at the Bryan's church, Immanuel Bible, were home-schooling. Today, despite the fact that the church has a good Christian school, over forty families are home-schooling. It was these children and their parents who made Brenda realize her stereotype was not accurate.

Karen Tanksley, of Mississippi, has set aside her career as a pediatrician in order to home-school her four children. Karen said, "I love it. And there are tremendous curriculums available." She describes a typical day:

> We're up at seven and we begin with a very practical course in home-economics! They fix breakfast, (even our six-year-old son can make scrambled eggs), sort the laundry, and clean the house.

After family devotions, I usually begin with the oldest, getting her started on a reading or a math workbook. Then I move on to the others. I don't have to hold them back the way I would in a classroom. When they finish one text, they go right on to the next. Our eight-year-old, for example, is in a fourth grade math text and is reading far beyond her level. She's finished the Laura Ingalls Wilder books and the Ramona series. They're all avid readers.

I can also seize their interests, the way I could not do if I had a classroom of kids. For example, if they became interested in Japan from our reading, we'd head for the library for books on Japan, and then have some hands-on experience back home with origami or stir-fry cooking. It's great fun, and all the time we're learning, the Lord is knitting us together.

The criticism that home-schooled kids will be behind their peers academically has been muffled by test results which show them to be 1.04 grades, on the average, above their grade level.[17] But another criticism to which home-schoolers are very sensitive is that they are isolating their children. Most involve their children in extra-curricular sports or arts. With home-schooling on the rise, every state has organizations which host curriculum fairs, competitions, and provide legal help.[18] Eighty-five percent of home-schoolers are Christians so there's a great deal of rapport and networking.[19]

Another criticism leveled at home-schoolers is that the mother doesn't have any time left for ministry outside the family. One mom from New Mexico gave this rebuttal:

> Home-schooling has refocused me, making me put my children before ministry—and actually that has been very healthy because before, the children got what was left. Home-schooling *does* take all of your time. But you don't have to stop ministering in the world. Part of raising our children in the way they should go means

discipling them in ministry. We deliver mobile meals weekly to shut-ins, and they've each "adopted a grandparent" through that. We write letters to legislators, bake cookies for prisoners, and pray for missionaries around the world. My kids and I are not hothouse Christians.

Most of the mothers at my retreats, whether they homeschooled or not, had caught the vision for building character in their children. Several mentioned, for example, that they wanted to help their children grow to be free of prejudice. I was moved by this testimony from a mother of three:

We long for our children to become lights in a world filled with hate and prejudice. We read lots of books to help with this goal, having recently finished the *All-of-a-Kind-Family* series, about daughters in a Jewish home. Our family has a ministry of hospitality. We're involved with befriending international students here in Denver. Having these people right at our dinner table with our children is helping our children to be free, we pray, of the prejudice which cripples our world.

Are Christians prejudiced? Twenty-five percent of the readers of *Ladies Home Journal* said they would find it intolerable if their child married someone from another race. How, I wondered, would the women at my retreats compare?

We weren't Christians when our daughter married a black man. He is a wonderful Christian man, but we could not accept him. We didn't go to the wedding and we cut them out of our lives.

Since receiving and growing in Christ, the greatest change in our lives is our acceptance of our son-in-law and the healing God has brought to our family.

A Nebraska woman

Is Our Lifestyle Free of Prejudice?

7 Pride and prejudice are cousins, sharing the trait of seeing oneself as better than others. And these cousins provide the drama in the book of Esther.

Mordecai and Haman: Pride and Prejudice

With Esther as Queen, her guardian, Mordecai, conducted his political business outside of the palace gate. Mordecai was not too fond of Xerxes, though he did warn him when guards were plotting to take his life. But the man Mordecai particularly despised was Haman, perhaps because as the right-hand-man of Xerxes, he flaunted his power.

Xerxes had commanded that the subjects of the kingdom bow down to Haman. There was nothing blasphemous about that, for as Dr. Frank E. Gaebelein comments, there are many scriptural examples of God's people prostrating themselves before kings or superiors (cf. 1 Sam. 24:8; 1 Kings 1:16). But Mordecai refused. His motive was probably pride, as the Targum suggests. "No self-respecting Benjamite," Gaebelein comments wryly, "would bow before a descendent of the ancient Amalekite enemy of the Jews!"[1]

Upon learning that Mordecai is a Jew, Haman fumed! He

ran to Xerxes and requested, not only that Mordecai be killed, but all Jews, including women and little children. With no regard for the sanctity of life and oblivious to the fact that his lovely wife is a Jewess, Xerxes agreed and gave Haman his ring to seal the decree. Pur (or lots) were thrown to decide upon the day of the slaughter, and providentially it landed on a day nearly a year away.

Pastor John Bronson compares Mordecai to the kid who is aghast by the avalanche he caused by taking the bottom apple out of a pyramid at the grocery store.[2] Mordecai tore his clothes, put on sackcloth and ashes, and wailed loudly outside the palace. When Esther learned of his distress, she was grieved for she loved him. Mordecai told Esther, through a messenger, to go to Xerxes on behalf of their people and plead for their lives. At first, Esther resisted, explaining that anyone who approached the king without being summoned would be put to death. Not only that, but she was unsure of Xerxes' feelings for her, for he has not asked her to come to his bed in over thirty days.

But then Mordecai said:

> Do not think that because you are in the king's house you alone of all the Jews will escape. For if you remain silent at this time, relief and deliverance for the Jews will arise from another place, but you and your father's family will perish. And who knows but that you have come to royal position for such a time as this? (Es. 4:13-14)

It's at this moment, when faced with death, that Esther saw God and eternity and changed from a reed which bent in the wind to an oak which stood tall in the gale. Her famous response is: "I will go to the king, even though it is against the law. And if I perish, I perish" (Es. 4:16). I'll return to Esther and her newfound maturity later, but for now, I'd like to talk about the pride and prejudice that brought about the near holocaust in Esther's day and still plagues our world.

Are Christians Prejudiced?

The media loves to portray Christians as bigots. While there are Christians who are bigots, studies show that those who attend church more than once a week are actually likely to be the least prejudiced.

Intriguingly, however, people who attend church only occasionally tend to be more prejudiced than either frequent attenders or the non churched. In *The Psychology of Religion*, the authors demonstrate their findings with this graph:[3]

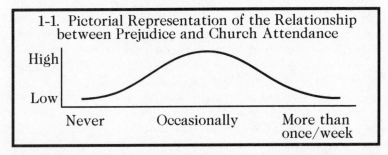

1-1. Pictorial Representation of the Relationship between Prejudice and Church Attendance

High

Low

Never   Occasionally   More than once/week

It's not too hard to understand why people who go to church occasionally may be prejudiced. I would agree with the researchers' explanation that casual church attendance is indicative more of the "American way of life" than of intrinsic faith. What is difficult to understand is why those who never go to church are less prejudiced than the casual attender, and in fact, only slightly more prejudiced than the frequent attender. The explanation the researchers give is that going to church frequently and not going to church at all are both deviants from the norm: therefore, this kind of person is more likely to think through his personal value system rather than simply adopting the prejudices of the culture.

It is encouraging to me to see that frequent church attenders are the least prejudiced.

The following graph contrasts the response of the readers of *Ladies Home Journal*[4] to the response of the women at my retreats to this question: "If your child were to marry someone of another race, which would be your response?"

	LHJ Readers	Retreat Women
(A) Accept it	25%	58%
(B) Be upset but accept it	50%	39%
(C) Find it intolerable	25%	3%

Again, this was a difficult question. Many women wrote, "I'd accept it if he/she was a believer!" Others, who chose B, hastened to explain, like this woman from Virginia:

> I don't think I'd be upset because of prejudice, but because they and their children would have an uphill battle in our society, a battle, which, in the optimism of youthful love, tends to be minimized. Yes, I'd probably be upset. But once the decision was made, I'd embrace them.

I think it's a tribute to the power of Christ that whereas 25 percent of *Ladies Home Journal* readers would find inter-racial marriage intolerable, only 3 percent of the women at my retreats would find it so.

Scripturally, we know that in Christ there is "neither Jew nor Greek, slave nor free, male nor female" (Gal. 3:28). One of the most dramatic Bible stories dealing with prejudice concerns Miriam and Aaron's negative reaction to the Ethiopian (and therefore probably black) woman that their brother, Moses, married. We are told the Lord's anger was kindled against them when they spoke against this woman and that Miriam became white as snow with leprosy. Aaron beseeches the Lord on behalf of his sister, admitting their sin. When Moses adds his plea to that of Aaron's, the Lord relents (Num. 12).

Anne, our Korean daughter, has experienced prejudice in Nebraska, even from children from Christian homes, though that is less common. Sometimes children will pull their eyes to make them look slanted when they look at Anne. Recently, a woman told me that her little Korean girl, in response to this kind of teasing, said, "Mommy, how would they feel if I went like this?" Then she proceeded to push her eyes in, squishing them and making them rounded. I told this story to Anne, and she collapsed in hysterical laughter. How easy it is to assume people are inferior simply because they are different!

Racial prejudice, however, is just one of many prejudices. Most of us are more likely to display prejudice in more subtle ways.

The More Subtle Prejudices

Vance Packard, in his book, *The Status Seekers*, has a challenging chapter titled: "The Long Road from Pentecostal to Episcopal."[5] Packard charges, with strong supporting evidence, that many Protestants choose their denomination for social reasons. At the top, he says, are Episcopalians. Here is some of his evidence:

> Two-thirds of Philadelphians who were in both the "Social Register" and "Who's Who" are Episcopalian. Three-quarters of Protestant wedding announcements involving socially prominent families in "The New York Times" showed the wedding occurred in Episcopal churches.
>
> Corporate executives are ten times as likely to list "Episcopal" as their religious preference as are Americans at large.[6]

Then Packard stair-steps down to Congregational, Presbyterian, Methodist, Lutheran, Baptist, and, finally, Pentecostal. (When Steve and I joined a Baptist church in Oregon, my grandmother was shocked. She said, "Dee! Don't you know that Baptist is two steps down from Methodist?") Catholics, Packard says, reflect every social class.

Lest I be misunderstood, I know and love committed Christians in every single one of these denominations. (And a few of the strongest Christians I know are Episcopalian!) Yet I think there is some validity in Packard's accusation that some folks are not choosing their church because it is helping them to grow spiritually, but rather because it is helping them move ahead socially.

I suspect that that is not true for most of the readers of this book, though it certainly doesn't hurt to ask if your church is helping you to grow spiritually, if you are being challenged to study and apply Scripture to your life.

A more relevant question, which is convicting to me, is "How *do* I relate to people who are not of my social class?" As I look at my own heart, I realize that I *am* most comfortable with people like me. I can become uncomfortable with the extremely sophisticated or the very unsophisticated. How sad! Instead of seeing Christ in them, I have a tendency to see their social standing. This subtle prejudice in my life feeds into church stratification.

Likewise, we can form cliques in our churches that are not too different from elementary school cliques. We can seek out only those of our own popularity, or of our own age (a weakness age-related classes amplify), despite the fact that Scripture exhorts the older to teach the younger.

When Jesus prayed that true believers would be one so that the world would believe that there really was something to Christianity, I believe He meant that we would be one despite our color, social standing, age, and denomination (See John 17:20-23.) Perhaps the prejudice that grieves Him the most is denominational backbiting. What joy it must give Him when He sees us loving and respecting one another despite the fact that we may prefer different styles of worshiping Him, from liturgy to the raising of our hands.

Perhaps you've heard the joke that in heaven we'll need to whisper outside the mansion for Baptists (or it could be Lutherans, or Catholics, or Evangelicals, or Charismatics) because they think they're the only ones there.

A good friend of mine whose full-time job is to coordinate volunteers for Lincoln, Nebraska's needy, told me:

God has stripped away my prejudice as women from "liberal" churches have come, eager to volunteer out of a desire to be obedient to Christ. I had prejudged them as not being believers, but often they put evangelicals to shame. I am learning to see Christ embodied in people from so many Christian denominations.

The research that I've done for this book has been illuminating some of the dark corners of prejudice in my heart. For again and again, I find that frequent attenders, *no matter the denomination,* are the ones who tend to be living the Christian life. And, to paraphrase James, a life of obedience is indicative of a life of faith (James 1:18). And if you ask: "Why would you attend a weak church frequently?" then I would answer: "Because you possess a heart that desires to worship God, and you will go, even if the environment is less than it should be."

Prejudice can also keep us from opening our hearts and lives to those who don't know Christ. The Lord showed me this sin in my life when we were living in Akron.

Prejudice against the Unsaved

I remember the sultry hot August day of the "Residents' Wives' Welcoming Tea." As I watched the women move about in their sundresses and shorts, sipping iced tea with lemon slices, I felt intimidated by their sophisticated ease.

We were told that at the next meeting, clubs would be formed, such as tennis and bridge. If we wanted to spearhead a new group, we were to bring a sign-up sheet and take responsibility for organizing it.

I had what I thought was a brilliant idea. I'd organize a Bible study and bring these pagan doctors' wives to Christ!

At that September meeting, I stood up. Though my knees were shaking, I smiled as I told them how interesting a beginners' Bible study could be. Then I passed around the sign-up sheet.

The sign-up sheet for bridge passed me. It had fifteen signatures! Arts and crafts had seventeen. Tennis had ten. Then my Bible study sheet returned. It had two signatures:

mine, and that of my Christian friend, Mary-Alice.

Driving home, I had some bitter thoughts. *Well, Lord, I tried. Obviously these women are just a bunch of worldly doctors' wives. Hardhearted. Interested only in material things. Unreachable.*

But deep inside I recognized the Spirit's soft prompting. My attitude was wrong. My pride had suffered a blow and now my prejudice was showing.

I didn't know these women. The Spirit brought to my remembrance my feelings before I trusted Christ. If a stranger had stood up and announced a Bible study, would I have gone? Probably not—not so much because I was hardhearted, but because I'd have been wary of someone I didn't know.[7]

So often, today, Christians do not befriend non-Christians. They allow them to remain strangers, even though studies show that it is very rare for a stranger to lead another stranger to Christ. Most people who come to Christ do so through the influence of someone who cared enough to become a genuine friend. Why are we content in our Christian cloister? Why do so few Christians venture out to befriend non-Christians? I think it is because we are afflicted with the same kind of subtle prejudice that I demonstrated in Akron.

That September day in Akron I realized two things. First, I needed to take the time and effort to really become friends with these women. Second, I needed help. If I were going to swim upstream, I needed someone to swim with me. God had given me that when my friend, Mary-Alice, signed the sheet. When Mary-Alice and I overcame our wounded pride, buried our prejudice, and began to work as a team, we experienced a tremendous power.

I'm going to tell you what happened with the doctors' wives in Akron—but first, I need to tell you why we must never underestimate our power as women.

At the crux of women's existence, the researchers contend, is the sense of relationship, the interconnectedness of people. . . . Women tend to see people as mutually dependent; men view them as self-reliant. Women emphasize caring; men value freedom.

Time[1]

What Is a Woman's Style of Ministry?

8 As I'm writing this chapter, I'm spending a restorative week with my family in my sister's log cabin in Door County, the peninsula of Wisconsin which juts out into Lake Michigan. It's been a stormy, windy week. The steady drum of rain on the logs and the rhythm of crashing waves mesmerizes us as we watch the fury from the cabin with awe. Now and then a lightning bolt will illuminate the whole sky and bay, as if God were turning the spotlight on His theater. The cedar and birch trees wave their branches like mad conductors orchestrating the whitecaps: "Higher. Louder. Now, crash!"

It would be cold and damp except for an enormous fire crackling in the cabin's great stone fireplace. We've cozied around it and read, played Scrabble, and conversed over roasted marshmallows. My twenty-one-year old nephew, Jimmy, is an expert fire builder. He carries in loads of logs, places them precisely so, and then squirts charcoal lighter fluid on the wet, smoldering logs. He steps back as the flame leaps dangerously high.

I watch my nephew with some fear for it was at this very fireplace that I had the worst accident of my life. When I was twelve, the fascination of the fire drew me, and I poked at the burning logs while wearing a long combustible bathrobe. The flames leapt and a spark landed on my bathrobe. Instantly I was engulfed in flame. I tugged wildly at the zipper, but it wouldn't budge. My grandmother heard my screams and rushed in. When she saw me, she grabbed a rag rug and wrapped it around me, smothering the flames.

We had no telephone in the cabin in those days, and Grandmother was alone with me, without a car. Afraid to leave me, she waited for my mother and aunt to return from their golf game while I writhed in pain. Hours later, though it seemed like days, they returned and rushed for the doctor who eased my pain with morphine. I spent the whole summer in the hospital and still have a few scars on the side of my torso reminding me not to play with fire. I have a deep appreciation for the power of fire, and the pain it can bring.

Yet this stormy week I'm glad for the fire, for the wonderful refuge it is from the storm. And likewise, I am aware of the good it can do.

Women are like logs in a fire which ignite other logs pressed close them. We have the same combustible power because, unlike men, intimacy is the very fabric of our lives.

Men Are Like the Grey Goose, Women Fly in Flocks

In *A Severe Mercy*, Sheldon Vanauken explains that the Grey Goose, if its mate is killed, flies on alone for life. And he, after his wife Davy died in their youth, has flown on alone.[2] Most men, researchers tell us, see themselves as standing alone and often work best alone.[2]

Most women, in contrast, see themselves as interdependent. They fly through life in flocks, leaning on one another for guidance and emotional support. Examples abound.

Psychiatrist Jean Baker Miller of Wellesley College says, "Women's sense of self and of worth is grounded in the ability to make and maintain relationships." When men attempt suicide, it's commonly over a feeling of incompetence, often related to work. When women attempt suicide, it's usually because of failures involving lovers, family, or friends.[3] Connection for women seems essential for life.

Sociolinguist Deborah Tannen, in *You Just Don't Understand: Men and Women in Conversation,* says men excel in "report talk": holding the floor in a monologue with stories or jokes. Women, on the other hand, excel in "rapport talk": a two-way conversation of matching experiences, affirmation, and questions to draw one another out and *connect.*[3]

Tannen also explains that men will drive around for thirty minutes rather than asking for directions because of their strong desire to maintain their self-sufficiency and independence. In contrast, women will quickly stop and ask, for it is a way of establishing connection, and *women like connection.*[4] (Perhaps the Israelites wandered in the wilderness for forty years because the men were in charge.)

Women executives prefer a teamwork approach rather than the masculine hierarchal style of leadership, explains Sally Helgesen in *The Female Advantage: Women's Ways of Leadership.*[5] They talk more frankly with employees, sharing rather than withholding information because they want input. They keep their office door open, literally, while a male executive is likely to keep it closed.

In my book *The Friendships of Women,* I included many examples that clearly demonstrate that we, as women, do see ourselves as part of a web of relationships. I was interested to see how men responded to my book when we studied it in a mixed Sunday School class. The first day of class we asked the men and the women to describe themselves in a few sentences. I was confident that most women would describe themselves in terms of relationships, whereas most men would describe themselves in terms of their jobs or hobbies. Each sex was following true to form, until we got to Ted Sabata. He said, "I'm married to Mary Jo, we have three children. . . . I've read Dee's book—and this is a set-up!"

The fact that women see themselves as part of a web of relationships, far more than men, is the central reason for our tremendous power. Women are extremely responsive to loved ones and then their combustible flame races through their relationships, for evil, or for good.

Zeresh and Esther: A Study in Contrasts

Zeresh was married to Haman, the Hitler of Esther's day, the man who plotted the demise of the Jews. Zeresh loved Haman, and was sensitive to his moods. When he sulked about the fact that Mordecai was still not bowing down to him, Zeresh responded to him. She had the power, at this point, to calm Haman, to allay his fury. Instead, without prayer and without thought, she said:

> Have a gallows built, seventy-five feet high, and ask the king in the morning to have Mordecai hanged on it. Then go with the king to dinner and be happy. (Es. 5:14)

Zeresh used her power foolishly, and it exploded in her face. Not only was Haman hung on his own gallows, but the ten sons Zeresh had borne and nurtured were hung on gallows as well.

Ruthie Thune, wife of the senior pastor of Omaha's Christ Community Church, told me that the book of Esther has made her more aware of her influence over her husband. She said:

> Sometimes Bob will come home from a church board meeting mildly upset. One of the members has been critical of him or the church. As Bob's main sounding board, I realize that the way I react will have a tremendous impact, not only on him, but on the whole church. If I believe the member's words have merit, I can gently stimulate Bob to consider them carefully. If I become angry as well, I contribute strength to Bob's initial resistance. So I am keenly aware of my need to be sensitive to God's still small voice.

Ruthie Thune is a wise woman. She understands both the power she has in relationships and also her need to draw upon the power of God. Had Zeresh been tuned in to God, she might have turned the tide of history, at least for her own family.

Esther, like Zeresh, was troubled when her loved ones were in distress. We are knit together with those we love. When they hurt, we hurt. The contrast, however, is that Esther was a believer, and her response is much more controlled. She knew she must have wisdom and help from God, and so she said to Mordecai:

> Go, gather together all the Jews who are in Susa, and fast for me. Do not eat or drink for three days, night or day. I and my maids will fast as you do. When this is done, I will go to the king, even though it is against the law. And if I perish, I perish (Es. 4:16).

Esther is a wonderful model for us in this passage. She responds to Mordecai, but at a cautious pace. She listens to him carefully and then draws upon her web of relationships, asking them to fast, and therefore, we assume, to pray. She doesn't want to move without the wisdom and the strength of God behind her. She understands that she has the power to ignite Xerxes for evil or for good.

The key to using our power for good, and not for evil is a keen sensitivity to the will of God, and a determination to draw upon His wisdom and power through the Word, prayer, and fasting.

Have Christian women today learned from Esther's lifestyle? Are Bible study, prayer, and fasting characteristic of our lifestyle?

Fasting, Prayer, and Christian Women

A study by the Barna Research Group revealed that only 18 percent of born-again Christians read the Bible daily.[6] The women at my retreats showed a higher level of commitment. Fifty percent had daily quiet times in which they read Scripture and prayed. Only 6 percent said they rarely or never had quiet times in contrast to Barna's findings of 23 percent.

It's much more common for Christian women, in contrast to Christian men, to meet together for study and prayer. Publishers have whole lines of study guides for women, but not for men. Retreats for women abound, but not for men. And because the friendships of women tend to be deeper and more intimate than the friendships of men, women, I believe, are more likely to pray together about their personal needs.

As I have matured in Christ, my relationships have changed. My closest friendships now are characterized by prayer. For example, I walk nearly every day with my friend Jean. We talk about our ministries, our loved ones, and our weaknesses — and then we pray. I bathe my loved ones in prayer, and I look for answers to our problems in the Word. And on the basis of testimonies from Christian women at my retreats, I do not think I am unusual.

Fasting, on the other hand, was not a discipline most women practiced. This was the response to my survey question:

> Do you fast to strengthen your prayer life?
> (A) Regularly 10% (B) Occasionally 5% (C) Rarely or never 85%

Although it's a very scriptural practice, and one which Jesus modeled, most Christian women, with the exception of charismatic women, do not seem to see the value of fasting. When I told my sister, Sally, who is charismatic and fasts two days a week, that 85 percent of the women at my retreats rarely or never fast, she said, "Wow. What a weapon they are missing!"

Although I am not a charismatic, I have learned much from them. Perhaps this is because the Lord has given me Sally and also some very positive experiences with charismatic women at my retreats. One of the desires of my heart is to see the wall fall between charismatic women and other evangelical women so that we will learn to see beyond our differences to our hearts, to love each other, and to learn from each other's lifestyles. Fasting is one discipline that charismatic women are teaching me to appreciate.

Often, when I call my sister Sally with a problem in my life, she'll pray with me, and occasionally she suggests a fast as well. Inwardly, I groan, yet I also have experienced the fruit of fasting. I'd like to share one experience with you.

When we moved to Nebraska, our son John was befriended by some older boys who drank. By the time he was sixteen, we were very concerned, and constantly lifting him up to the Lord. I drew upon my web of relationships the Christmas of 1984 and pleaded with our friends to pray for John.

Shortly after that, I remember fasting for John, and I think Sally fasted with me. A few days later, I received a call from our youth pastor asking if a Nebraska football player could spend the night in our home. I agreed readily, though I was not familiar with the name Travis Turner. But when I told John, his eyes widened and he said: *"Travis Turner* is going to sleep here?"

Travis was God's messenger to John for he stayed up with our son until two in the morning, talking to him about his walk with God. A week later John came to us and said:

> I'm sorry for the way I've been living my life. I'm recommitting my life to Christ. I'm going to make new friends and pray for a godly girl. I'm going to quit my job and become active in the youth group. And I'm going to memorize *The Sermon on the Mount* so that I can walk the kind of walk Travis Turner walks.

And God empowered John to do as he had committed. His turn-around was quick, dramatic, and complete.

That was my first experience with Esther's plan of fasting and drawing upon my web of relationships. Since that time, I've had several opportunities to speak to charismatic women, who seem to do this frequently.

The Power of Praying and Fasting Together

In Austin, Texas, I spoke at Hope Chapel, a very alive, quite sophisticated, charismatic church. One of the pastors' wives,

Joyce Tait, explained to me that Hope had experienced revival after the pastors had called the congregation to a month of fasting and prayer, which stretched to three months. She said:

> It was a time of real repentance, and a turning point concerning our vision of Austin. It all happened in God's marvelous fullness of time, and so many doors were opened. The congregation was filled with a desire to reach out to the community, and many ministries were begun and are still thriving today. Members became involved by working with The Salvation Army, a food pantry, and work among the very poor. We've hired a new pastor, "Pastor of Mercy Ministries." Literally, hundreds have come to know the Lord as a result of this corporate experience of prayer and fasting.

When I spoke at Hope, I told the story of Ruth, and of how her friends had interceded for her in prayer because she had been barren for ten years. Merry Klonower, of Hope, identified with Ruth, and told her story, a few months later, at a wonderfully compassionate service which their church held for infertile couples. I'd like to share parts of Merry's story with you (available on tape from Hope Chapel[7]) because it demonstrates the power of women through fasting and prayer, and because sharing it may help to break down the wall that I see between charismatics and other evangelicals. Merry began her story by saying:

> About seven years ago Mark and I suffered a late miscarriage. Until that time I hadn't known if I wanted children, but after that, I knew, with all of my being, that I wanted children.
>
> Following that experience we were unable to get pregnant. Doctors did what they could, but it was clear that if we were going to have children, it was going to be up to God. Prayer and fasting had been a part of my Christian walk for over ten years, and so now I called upon

God for help and for wisdom in dealing with my
barrenness.

My sister has two beautiful children by adoption and
so we were very open to adoption. We began to ask the
Lord if we were to adopt. It surprised us, but God's
answer was a very clear: "No."

As the Book of Esther demonstrates, and as others will
testify, fasting can help you discover God's will on an issue.
God gave Esther wisdom after her time of fasting and prayer.
And God showed Merry and Mark that they were not to
adopt, but to wait. I wish you could hear the emotion in
Merry's voice as she said to Hope's congregation: "I want you
to know that if you know someone who can't have children—
they *are* hurting. And it's a grief that time does not ease."

As God refined Esther through pain, He also refined Merry.
She said:

> God taught me so much through those years of suffering
> that I can honestly tell you, if I had it to do over again, I
> would do it. There were things God worked in me that
> He could not work in any other way.

Merry asked herself some questions during that time of
waiting with which many Christian women will identify, wom-
en who are waiting for a husband, or a healing, or, as in
Merry's case, a baby. Those questions, Merry said with a
trembling voice, were:

> Do I trust You, God, and do I love You—even if You
> never give me the desire of my heart?
> Are You still God—and are You still good—even if I
> never have a child?

After wrestling with God, as Jacob did, Merry finally laid
her desire for a child down, and said, "Yes, God, I trust You."
Refined through the pain, Merry said, with conviction:

I truly knew that I trusted God, that He loved me, and that He was only going to do what was best for me. Either He would give me a child, or He would use the pain to transform me into the image of His son. Coming to the point of trusting Him, whatever He chose, has transformed my entire life. A miracle took place in me — a rebirth, though I'd been a Christian many years.

I appreciated Merry's honesty as she said:

Over ten years, Mark and I were given three or four prophecies that we would have a child — but I didn't always believe them. There were times when I just couldn't receive those words.

Merry heard from the Lord directly early one September morning:

I was lying in bed when I heard the Lord say: "Merry, get your house in order. You are going to have a baby, and it's going to be soon."

Merry's reaction was, "Soon? Well, with the Lord, who knows what 'soon' means!"

A few weeks later there was a retreat at her church and Merry didn't plan to go. During the morning of the retreat, two of Merry's friends felt strongly that she should come. They went into a back room and prayed that she would come in the afternoon. Merry said that her job had been very demanding and she didn't really want to come, but she came. (Never underestimate the power of women who pray, agreeing together in Jesus' name.) The last session of the day was a healing service, and as soon as it began, Merry sensed that the Lord was telling her she was going to be prayed for. She described her feelings:

I don't know if any of you have had ongoing things that

you've been prayed for, but after a while you think, "I don't want people to pray for me one more time."

But sure enough, someone stood up and said, "I have a word that there is a woman here with scarring—and she's barren. Is there somebody out there?"

I couldn't deny it, so with a sigh of resignation, I raised my hand.

Merry said that there was a quiet time of prayer. A prophecy was given that Merry would have a child by that time, September 17, the next year.

In December Merry conceived Sarah. Sarah's due date was September 13 though she was born August 23. Reflectively, Merry said:

> Mark and I are convinced that it took every single prayer, every word of prophecy, for Sarah to be born. This was a spiritual battle, and the prayers and words that were spoken had to take place for that battle to be won. I get up every day and look at my little girl and I see what a miracle she is. I know God is faithful. I know God desires to do miracles. And I would ask you to be faithful in participating in those miracles for people, by praying, and by fasting.

Sometimes I'm hesitant to tell stories like this, for God doesn't always give the barren woman children, or cure people from cancer, or turn wayward children around. Sometimes, despite intense prayer and fasting, He still says, "No." Yet He is always faithful; He does all things well in His time. And personally, if I have teamed together with friends for prayer and fasting and He has not opened the door, I have a greater peace about the difficulty of my circumstances.

A postscript to Merry's story illustrates this point. Her friend, Dixie Stanforth, has not yet been able to conceive, despite years of fasting and prayer. Dixie is trusting God, however, even if He never gives her the desire of her heart.

The prayers of her friends, she feels, have not returned void, but have strengthened her to face whatever God has planned for her, and have enabled her to live a fruitful life. She tells about attending Merry's shower for Sarah.

> It was such a wonderful time of fellowship and rejoicing over the long awaited miracle that was Sarah. After all the gifts were opened, we had a time of thanksgiving for Merry. Merry shared from Psalms, and that was followed by some loving and powerful prayer on my behalf, and on the behalf of another woman there. We became true sisters, rejoicing with those who rejoice, and weeping with those who weep.

What a strong sense of teamwork! And teamwork is characteristic of the way Christian women minister.

Teamwork

Author Joy Dawson, commenting on the story of Esther and Mordecai, has observed that neither Esther nor Mordecai could have made it alone. Joy compares it to a seesaw, or to a game of Ping-Pong and says the fun begins only when both partners are moving![8] The following diagram demonstrates how the dramatic teamwork of Esther and Mordecai fulfilled God's sovereign purposes.

I found it interesting, as I interviewed chairwomen from women's ministries across this country, how often the vision was given to several women—the ministry was conceived and born through a team. This was the story when I interviewed women from Mother's Hour in Salina, Kansas; and MUMS (Mothers Uplifting Mothers) in Boca Raton, Florida; and M & M's (Moms Need Moms) in Albuquerque, New Mexico. National organizations, like Mothers in Touch (a prayer group for schools) and MOPS (Mothers of Preschoolers), likewise reflect the interdependent nature of women.

All this supports Joy Dawson's suggestion that we need to be very alert to "the ministry link" when God gives us a

The Teamwork of Mordecai and Esther

Mordecai learns of the plan to annihilate the Jews, tears his clothes, and puts on sackcloth and ashes, but can go only as far as the king's gate (Es. 4:1-2).

Esther sends clothes and a messenger to find out why Mordecai is grieving (Es. 4:4-5).

Mordecai confronts Esther through the messenger, asking her to go to Xerxes (Es. 4:13-14).

Esther asks Mordecai to gather the Jews for a three day fast and says she and her maids will do the same (Es. 4:16).

Mordecai carries out Esther's instructions (Es. 4:17).

Esther goes to Xerxes and invites him to a private banquet (Es. 5:5-6).

Xerxes is afflicted with insomnia and reads in his chronicles of how years earlier, Mordecai saved his life. He honors Mordecai and then Mordecai returns to his watchful place outside the palace gate (Es. 6).

On the second day of feasting, Esther asks Xerxes to spare her life and the lives of her people. When Xerxes agrees, Esther tells him she is related to Mordecai, and Xerxes allows Esther to give Mordecai a position of authority (Es. 7–8).

friend. Joy points out that just as God used Mordecai and Esther as a team, so may He have a sovereign purpose when He gives you a friend. He may be linking you for prayer, or for a short-term ministry, or, as in marriage, for a lifetime ministry.[9]

This takes me back to the story I began in the last chapter, of how God linked me with Mary-Alice the day I tried to interest the residents' wives in Akron in a Bible study. If you remember, I sent around a sign-up sheet, and it came back like this:

BEGINNERS' BIBLE STUDY

Sign here for an interesting study of the Gospel of Mark! We'll have good discussions over coffee. Baby-sitting. Thursdays at 9:30 A.M.

1. Dee Brestin	6.	11.
2. Mary-Alice Baldwin	7.	12.
3.	8.	13.
4.	9.	14.
5.	10.	15.

I believe Mary-Alice was my "ministry link." For the next year we concentrated on befriending women whom we met in the groups that had inspired much better sign-ups: arts and crafts and bridge. It took time to really be a friend, and nurturing two friendships each was about all Mary-Alice and I could do. Therefore it seems clear we needed each other; neither of us would have been successful in gathering enough women for a Bible study that next year had we worked alone.

I hadn't played bridge since I was a non-Christian, but I liked the game and it seemed a logical place to start. I remember calling Lee and asking her if there was still room in the bridge group. They were short one, as only fifteen had signed up. We laugh now at how she responded. She said, "Dee, you are an answer to prayer!"

Because I am not a night person, I found going out every other Tuesday night and staying up late difficult. I also struggled with the hospital gossip which dominated the conversations. I had to fight both the temptation to participate and the temptation to squelch them with a "holier than thou" comment. I drank coffee to stay awake and didn't participate much in the conversation. I began to wonder what I was really accomplishing.

One rainy night I came home and sat in our dark living room. My family was fast asleep, but I, with caffeine running through my veins, would be long in joining them. I began questioning the Lord. "Is this a wild goose chase? Or are you really leading me to spend my time this way?" I waited for His answer, and in the still of the night, He gave me a peace, and I sensed I was to seek a closer relationship with Lee and with Ann.

I genuinely liked them both. Ann and I had coffee together. Lee and I went Christmas shopping. We had several in-depth conversations and God was breaking down my prejudice as I found myself liking and respecting these women. Lee, for example, told me that after two sons, she had prayed for a girl. (I hid my astonishment by nodding and smiling.) She seemed overwhelmed at the miracle of her daughter. She was also involved in mobile meals, taking food to shut-ins. (*How can you be interested in that?* I thought. *I'm the one who is spiritual around here!*) But the fact is, Lee *did* have a spiritual hunger, a mustard seed of faith, and God knew all along she was going to be His—He'd known it from before the foundation of the world.

This is humbling for me to reflect on. It reminds me of Mordecai's advice to Esther. He said that if she remained silent, God would find another vehicle, but he believed that she was where she was for a purpose, "for such a time as this" (Es. 4:14). In the same way, Mary-Alice and I were in the right place at the right time, but we certainly were not God's only options.

Yet He gave us the privilege of being used, as a team. For

the next September, when we tried again to have a Bible study, God gave us success. Five women who'd never been to Bible study before, whom we'd spent the year befriending, agreed to give it a try. A few came to know the Lord and enthusiastically began inviting their friends. Eventually, like so many rabbits, we began to multiply. When their husbands finished their residencies, many moved to new cities and began studies of their own. Five years later, I was aware of six studies being led by women who'd come to know the Lord while living in Akron.[10]

The Dreams God Puts in Willing Hearts

Once you've experienced the excitement of working as a team within the sovereignty of God, you thirst for more. When Steve went into private practice with a group of Christian orthopedic surgeons in Kearney, Nebraska, I had long since given up my dream of arts and crafts or a house on the Pacific Ocean. (Do you think it's part of the Lord's sense of humor that He placed us as far from either ocean as possible?) I had a new dream. I wanted to see an interdenominational network of women's Bible studies form in Kearney. I could see God drawing women from every church in town—churches that trusted the Scriptures and preached Christ, and churches that didn't. I believe God put that dream in my heart, for when we moved to Kearney, it fell together as easily as a child's five-piece puzzle.

First, I met Shell Ramey. I met her the very morning I'd prayed for a woman friend. I sat next to her at a coffee for the mothers of kindergartners, and I was drawn. She had depth, telling me of a book she was reading, and I sensed an interest in spiritual things. I determined to get to know her better.

What I didn't know was that Shell was a brand-new Christian. The year before, her heart had been softened by the death of her dad and struggles in her second marriage. Her neighbor, Karen Carlson, gently suggested that she listen to Chuck Swindoll, who was doing a series on marriage. Karen said, "We can all use a little help with our marriages.

So God put the four of us together: Shell, Karen, a woman named Renee Brodine, and myself, representing three key churches in Kearney. When I shared my dream, they caught it quickly, because God had put them in such a place for such a time and they were open. We each invited friends from our churches and began with one study group.

We met in a home and my son, J.R., took his study hall and lunch break and came home from high school to take care of the children. J.R. was great, taking as many children as we gave him down in the basement, but we knew this was a temporary and less than satisfactory arrangement.

The second year I invited Phyllis Henderson to "Sonrise Women's Studies," and she said, "I think God wants me to head up a ministry with the children." And she formed "Sonrise Children's Bible Club," which began to use the facilities of a church while the women continued to meet in homes.

As we prayed, church doors opened to us. We've had our fall kick-offs in nearly every large Protestant and Catholic church in town. Today, eight years later, we have 175 women in twelve studies meeting at many different times—and we have 60 children in Bible Club. God has transferred the reins to another woman, Maurita Barthelman, because it's His dream—not mine. Many women and children have come to Christ and grown in Him, and I know God is glorified by women from different denominations growing to love one another.

Believe me, this is a lot more exciting than arts and crafts or a house on the Pacific Ocean! This realized dream is bearing fruit for eternity.

The dream of helping people is a dream I heard again and again as I talked to Christian women throughout this country. I'm praying that as I tell you of some of their realized dreams, God will ignite a dream in your heart.

True evangelical faith cannot lie dormant.
It clothes the naked.
It feeds the hungry.
It comforts the sorrowful.
It shelters the destitute.
It serves those that harm it.
It binds up that which is wounded.
It has become all things to all men.

Menno Simons (1539)
(One of the founders of the Mennonites)

Are We Making a Difference in Our World?

9 It's exciting to reflect back on the ways God changed my lifestyle—right away! One change was an overwhelming desire to serve Him. But with the limited vision of a child, all I could think of doing was church work. Compelled, I knocked on my pastor's study door and enlisted. He put me to work, two afternoons a week, as a secretary. So while one-year-old J.R. pushed his giraffe-walker up and down the church halls, I typed. (My pastor was obviously desperate.)

Most of the women at my retreats are involved in some ministry in their local church. Many wrote of the joy it gave them, like this twenty-five-year-old from Nebraska:

Choir is a full-time Sunday and Wednesday commitment. When I see our congregation worshiping, really worshiping, a warmth spreads through me.

Or this thirty-seven-year-old from Connecticut:

I've taught sixth-grade girls for twelve years. Because I'm single, I have time to pray, to take girls out individually for frozen yogurt, to dream up ways to get them to memorize long passages (this year I had seven memorize all of Philippians), and to involve them in ministry: helping in the nursery, or with summer backyard clubs, or sitting for free for single moms. Seeing them blossom into godly young women means so much to me—and many now tell me I was a significant factor in that growth. I feel like my life is counting.

The local church is and always will be the backbone of the body of Christ, and I believe every Christian should serve in it in some way; however, as I've grown in Christ, I've seen the importance of expanding my definition of ministry beyond church work.

Beyond the Church Doors

Steve took a year of training in Fargo, North Dakota, and we sat under the excellent teaching of Greg Scharf, Pastor of Salem Evangelical Free Church. I remember the Sunday he preached on Isaiah 58, a convicting passage about believers who were having daily quiet times, were fasting, and were active in church work, yet had rebellious hearts! Isaiah's message penetrated my heart that Sunday morning:

Is not this the kind of fasting I have chosen:
to loose the chains of injustice,
and untie the cords of the yoke,
to set the oppressed free and break every yoke?
Is it not to share your food with the hungry
and to provide the poor wanderer with shelter—when
you see the naked, to clothe him,
and not to turn away from your own flesh and blood?
(Isa. 58:6-7)

As I sat transfixed, Pastor Scharf said:

The besetting sin of evangelicals is that we have rede-
fined obedience in our own terms instead of God's
terms. We have limited it simply to the things we are
already doing, to "church things," rather than including
all kinds of other things.[1]

It is true that church people are much more likely to volunteer to help the less fortunate than are unchurched people.
New Woman, a liberal secular magazine, found that 25 percent
of their readers were involved in volunteer work.[2] In contrast
George Gallup has found that 60 percent of those affiliated
with a religious institution become volunteers. And those who
frequently go to church, no matter the denomination, volunteer most of all.[3]

And though we've a long way to go, there's been growth
among evangelicals. Evangelical leaders such as Francis
Schaeffer and John Stott warn against divorcing God from the
whole of life. John Stott says: "According to the Old Testament prophets and the teaching of Jesus, God is very critical
of "religion," if by that is meant religious services divorced
from real life, loving service, and the moral obedience of the
heart."[4] Many are realizing that to win people to Christ we
must meet their needs, treating them as whole people, as
Jesus did, and not just as souls to be won. Many churches
have ministries to encourage their members with this. At Immanuel Faith Church in Springfield, Virginia a woman, Gene
Hall, is a *full-time volunteer* coordinating women's ministries.
One of those ministries is "A Clothing Exchange," where the
community is invited twice yearly to come and take what they
need. At the Rancho Bernardo Community Church in the San
Diego area, sixty-five people come weekly to pair with indi-
viduals from the community who wish to learn to read English. At Heights Cumberland Presbyterian Church in Albuquerque, couples with solid marriages take other couples who
would like free premarital counseling through a six-week
course. Through these ministries and others like them, people
are finding Christ.

Hospitality

Many women have a knack for hospitality. Esther did. Perhaps she was familiar with the saying that the way to a man's heart is through his stomach because she wined and dined Xerxes twice before she made her plea for her people.

There's something about inviting people into your home and breaking bread with them that binds you together. Jesus is very clear, however, that He particularly wants us to invite those who are somehow in need, not just our rich friends and relatives who will invite us back (Luke 14:12-14).

Here are a few testimonies from women who are using hospitality to minister to those in need:

A sixty-five-year-old from Maryland:

> I open my home to 50-100 people yearly, particularly Haitian women. Women are treated very poorly in Haiti, and it's a thrill to see their faces light up as they learn how special they are to God.

A thirty-six-year-old from New Mexico:

> We tried everything to have children. God had to knock me over the head to show me He had different plans. Now, after fostering 26 children and adopting two of those, (and trying for two more) I see how perfect His way is. I was a physically and sexually abused child. Christ is in the process of healing me, and part of that healing is reaching out to these children, many of whom have been abused and neglected, with the unconditional love of Christ. Right now we have six children in our home.

A thirty-two-year-old from Wisconsin:

> About six years ago a college girl in our youth group moved in with us during her pregnancy. After that we

called a local agency and told them we'd be willing to be on their list. We've had three other girls since then, including a German girl. Before this, our hospitality was very sporadic, but I like having someone move right in because then I'm sure we're doing something. It's too easy, otherwise, to be lazy, like the servant in Matthew 25:26.

I'm convinced that God brings people across our path for a purpose. Yet so often I've been like the Priest or the Levite in the parable of the Good Samaritan. I've been so busy with my church responsibilities that I've stepped over the broken and bleeding person who lay across my path.

I remember when I met the mother of one of our daughter's first-grade classmates. I wasn't too interested in getting involved in her life. I felt my stomach tighten when Sally's teacher caught me and proposed:

I'd like to introduce you to Chinda, Mittra's mother. They've just moved here from Thailand and are having a rough time. Chinda is adjusting to a new country, language, marriage, and baby. Her husband, an American man thirty years her senior, had a stroke last week. Chinda is trying to manage their restaurant, visit her husband in the hospital, and take care of two little girls. She could really use a friend! Would you like to meet her?

I thought, *No! This woman sounds like she'll swallow me alive!* But, I smiled and said, "I'd love it!"

A delicate beauty with a baby in her arms, Chinda looked like a child herself. My offer was a limited one. I said, "Perhaps Mittra would like to come and play with Sally sometime."

Chinda's dark eyes brightened, and in broken English she said: "Thanks! Okay! Mittra go now with you!"

My involvement in Chinda's life snowballed quickly, for

when I walked Mittra to her door that night, Chinda met me and said: "I go visit my husband in Omaha for two days. Girls stay with you. Okay?"

I thought, *My fears, exactly.* But to Chinda, I said, "I'd love to have the girls!"

The baby was fussy, the weekend long. I was trying to get ready for Thanksgiving company the following week. With Christmas around the corner, I felt resentful of this unexpected burden. (Priests and Levites are especially busy during the holidays.)

Chinda's husband was released from the hospital but needed much care. One night, when Chinda came for Mittra, she stood on the porch, snow swirling behind her. She said, "It's cold. Can I come in?" Embarrassed by my lack of hospitality, I quickly invited her to take off her coat and sit by the fire.

Chinda was direct: "My husband sad. He not want to live. He think he never going to be well. I scared what he maybe do."

I didn't know what to say. We sat there watching the fire, and I took her hands in mine and told her I was sorry. Finally, I walked her to the door and told her I'd pray for her. I truly intended to pray about what my part should be—I didn't realize that time was running out. Chinda's parting look haunted me. "Won't you do more?" it pled.

The next morning in Bible study, we took prayer requests. My breath was knocked out of me when one woman said:

> The police were in our neighborhood last night. A man tried to kill himself. But his wife, a young woman from Thailand named Chinda, wrestled the gun away and ran next door and called the police.

After the study, I drove to see my dear friend, Shell. Under conviction, I wept as I drove. I had stepped over a bleeding traveler in my path. Concentrating only on my spiritual schedule, I had ignored God's leading and worked at cross purposes with Him.

When I got to Shell's house, I sat in the car for a moment, trying to collect myself. Shell saw me and came out. Seeing my tears, she opened the car door and knelt down, "Dee, what's wrong?"

I confessed my sin to Shell that day, telling her how I'd shut up my compassion for one God had brought to me. When I told Shell that I'd been afraid Chinda's needs would swallow me up, Shell responded as is typical for good women friends. She offered to help me. As a team, we went to see Chinda and wholeheartedly offered our help.

During the next few months, Shell and I spent lots of time with Chinda and her daughters. Once I let down my guard, I began to love them and the resentment I felt began dissipating. I remember the night Chinda cooked Thai dishes for the church youth group. Our kitchen was filled with love and laughter.

Because of her husband's illness, the financial needs were great. One night Chinda said to me, simply: "In America when you need money, you have garage sale. Okay?"

I said, "Yes, Chinda, but February isn't a very good month for garage sales in Nebraska."

Her dark eyes widened: "I need this garage sale now." Though her request seemed impractical, still, I wasn't going to refuse her this time.

Shell and I and our Sonrise Bible study group spent the next several nights marking Chinda's family belongings.

The day before the garage sale I said, "Chinda, let's pray about this garage sale. I'm going to ask God to help people look in the paper for the ad, and I'm going to ask for nice weather."

Chinda asked, simply: "Will your God hear you?"

I hesitated. Then, to Chinda, I said: "Yes."

And silently to God, I breathed, "PLEASE!"

The next morning was like a day in May. A steady stream of people came from morning to late afternoon. Chinda made the money she needed, and she said, "Your God hear you!" Shell and I smiled, our hearts full.

Chinda came to the Lord that April. One day, when Mittra was over playing with Sally, she said to me, "Why is Mommy so different?" And I led Mittra to the Lord.

I wish I could tell you today that Chinda is living today for the Lord. But she's not. Her husband died a few years later and Chinda married an unbeliever. And though she said she'd never forget the miracles God had done in her life, she seems to have. Chinda has moved away and doesn't write to me. However, Mittra writes to Sally and still longs to walk with the Lord. I rejoice in that and I pray for Chinda.

The Lord is teaching me that all He expects from me is faithfulness. One woman from Chicago has also learned this lesson. She wrote:

> It takes so much energy, patience, and compassion to get involved with people's messed-up lives. I visit women in prison, and I've been a halfway house for several as well. Sometimes it's all I hoped for, but just as often they go back to the bottle or back to a sexually immoral lifestyle. And then they push me out of their lives. But I keep on because I know God wants me to, and the fruit is His concern, not mine.

The Example of God's Commitment to Us

God wants us to reach out to those He puts across our path. Though it hurts when it doesn't succeed, I know God understands that hurt, for He's been there. In Ezekiel 16, the prophet compares God's hospitality to us to finding a baby in a ditch and cleaning her up, raising her and clothing her—yet having her turn her back on Him. Philip Yancey comments on that parable, imagining God's feelings:

> I'll tell you how I feel! I feel like a rejected parent. I find a baby girl lying in a ditch, near death. I take her home and make her my daughter. I clean her, pay for her schooling, feed her. I dote on her, clothe her, hang jewelry on her. Then one day she runs away, I hear reports of

her debased life. When my name comes up, she curses me. . . . I feel betrayed, abandoned, cuckolded."[5]

Yet as God continues reaching out to man, despite disappointing experiences, He wants us to follow in His steps. He doesn't insist that hospitality always bear fruit, but that we always be faithful. And sometimes, that persistence will bear fruit, if we don't grow weary.

When we went through the adoption process, Barbara Kim, our caseworker, talked to us very seriously about our commitment. She said:

> Adopting is just like giving birth. You don't return the child if you don't like him or if things aren't turning out like you'd hoped. This is a permanent commitment with no guarantees.

Barb is perfectly suited for her job as a caseworker because she was adopted as an older child. Her Korean parents rejected her because she was female and born lame. She was not permitted in their home after her brother was born, though she was just two. She lived with a grandmother until she was taken to an orphanage. At ten she was adopted into an American home, but the adoption failed. She was put into a foster home. Barb tells how she behaved in that foster home:

> They were a loving Mennonite family—genuine Christians. But I didn't believe anybody could really love me—my self-esteem was so low. One night I put their love to the test: I climbed up on top of the roof and screamed so all the neighbors could hear: "I hate you! I don't want to live here anymore!" I hoped they would bring me down and tell me that they loved me even if I hated them and that they were committed to me. But instead, because they were gracious people who misread my cries, they told me that if I didn't want to live with them, I didn't have to. I left, but it broke my heart.

Barbara today is a lovely Christian woman with a heart of compassion for unwanted children. A single parent with two natural children, she has recently adopted an older Brazilian boy from a troubled background. She's committed to him and she tells adoptive parents to be committed to their children, even if they don't seem to appreciate it. "Don't expect," she warns, "for them to be eternally grateful to you for bringing them out of an orphanage. Most kids aren't like that."

We're one of the fortunate families apparently, for our little Anne is continually thanking God for her adoption and for us. But should there come a day when she's not, I'll cling to Barb's wisdom and God's example of commitment to me.

In addition to extending hospitality to the hurting, Isaiah says believers should be involved in working for justice, in breaking the cords which bind the oppressed.

Working for Justice

Again and again women told me they were involved in the pro-life movement: that they voted pro-life, that they participated in demonstrations, that they were writing their congressmen. One woman said that, coming home from the Washington, D.C. pro-life rally, the people in her bus, who were unrelated, broke into "How Majestic Is Your Name!" Here are a few other testimonies:

New Mexico:
I used to be active in the pro-choice movement. While there are many who honestly believe they are helping women, others are fueled by guilt, as I was. It wasn't until I received Christ's forgiveness that I was able to see that my abortion was the taking of a human life. Last Sunday I participated in a "Life Chain" of 5,000 people stretching for ten miles through Albuquerque. What a change for me!

Maryland:
I'm a nurse and have offered my time to local high

schools to talk about prenatal care. I show them slides of babies in the womb, and tell them exactly what is involved in an abortion. These are important aspects of education that are censored by pro-choice advocates. I don't make a pro-life statement, but I do educate them concerning the facts. It's not fair for them to discover these things after they've had an abortion.

A few women at my retreats were involved in other issues. Jane Gronewold, an Omaha mother, told me that once a month she meets with other young moms to write letters to congressmen, using resources such as material from *Concerned Women of America* or Focus on the Family's *Citizen* magazine. They call their group "PALS" (Prayers and Letters). Jane said:

> We knew we should be writing letters, but we admitted we weren't. Meeting together is fun, and we get a lot accomplished. One woman gives us some direction, and then we pray and write.

Many Christian women are involved with "Moms in Touch" and pray together for their children in the public schools. I am convinced that prayer is key in the battle against decay in our public schools and also in the battles against pornography and abortion. These are, indeed, spiritual battles. In addition, I believe that we must do all we can to integrate mercy with our message. I think the reason people listened to Mother Teresa when she spoke out against abortion was because her lifestyle of mercy demanded a hearing.

My husband and I, like many Christians in many communities, have worked hard to influence public school administrators to adopt an abstinence curriculum and to stay away from death and dying and New Age curricula. After five years of prayer, hard work, and enormous amounts of time, we seem to have failed. I know there could have been more prayer, though there was much; I know there were lost tempers, though most behaved admirably. When we're trying to make a difference in our world and we seem to have failed, we have to cling to His promise that our work in the Lord is not in vain. Though we missed our target, He has encouraged our hearts through showing us some fruit: changes in smaller, more conservative outlying communities who watched our debate; changes in our children, who participated in our discussions; and changes in our lives, as we are refined through fire.

I am not going to stop sowing my seed because of this experience, though I may look for more fertile ground. I have taken Solomon's wisdom to heart:

> Sow your seed in the morning,
> and at evening let not your hands be idle,
> for you do not know which will succeed,
> whether this or that,
> or whether both will do equally well (Ecc. 11:6).

Ministry-Oriented Careers

Women in general often have careers that could be ministry-oriented, such as nursing and teaching. Some Christians are using these careers very wisely. Take, for example, this testimony from a Nebraska labor and delivery nurse:

> When I teach Lamaze, I hand out a sheet of verses—scriptural preparation for birth. I tell them I'll pray for them and talk about God's blessing after they deliver. If something goes wrong, I'll go to them—sometimes I'll just sit and cry. I've also had girls live with me during their pregnancy and then I've been their labor coach at the hospital. Because I'm a working mom, I don't have much time for other ministries, and I'm thankful I can do this in my job.

Or this Colorado fifth grade public school teacher:

> The First Amendment protects the students' freedom to speak about their faith. I encourage that by reading

books like *The Lion, The Witch, and The Wardrobe* and asking them about the symbolism. I invite them into my home each Christmas, making it clear on the invitation that it is voluntary and that I'm going to be talking about the real meaning of Christmas. Most come. I give my testimony and an opportunity to respond. Many do.

The Unique Opportunity for Single Women

It's very evident to me after doing the research for this book that Christian wives and mothers pour themselves into their families, sometimes to the exclusion of the outside world.

(I was impressed by the moms who saw the importance of modeling ministry to their children and found ways to do that without neglecting them: like visiting nursing homes with them, or shut-ins; or teaching their Awana group.)

Seeing the tremendous energy expended on family gave me a new appreciation for the unique opportunity that single women, or women whose children are grown, have to advance the kingdom of God. Francis Bacon put it like this: "A single life doth well . . . for charity will hardly water the ground where it must first fill a pool."[7]

Are single women using their reservoir of time and energy to "water the ground?" Some are, but many are stumbling over a unique obstacle in our American Christian culture.

In a valid attempt to strengthen the faltering family in our country, it's easy to simultaneously communicate the error that the single life is a lesser calling. Research of Evangelical women conducted by Patricia Ward and Martha Stout revealed that most of these women went to college to prepare for a career, but with an understanding that they would marry before or soon after graduation. This results, among those who do not marry, not only in a feeling of failure over not finding a mate, but in a lack of confidence in their abilities to minister alone.[8] This was expressed in my survey forms. One twenty-five-year-old from Virginia, said: "I feel it's hard to serve because it's hard for me to become involved by myself."

I discovered a lack of contentment, a frustration, among

many of the Christian singles at my retreats. Some of them seemed almost angry at my asking if they were freer to minister than their married friends. Many were grieving that they had not found a man to love them, that they'd been denied the dream of their hearts. I can understand that, and I believe they should be free to grieve. Many of these women, I think, are not "called to singleness" but are single because we live in a fallen world where things are not as they should be. I don't believe that it's God's perfect plan for Christian women to outnumber men, or for widows to outnumber widowers five to one.

Sin, whether it is our own, or simply universal sin, can put us in extremely difficult positions. That's what happened to Esther. Yet God can work within those situations to bring good out of them. He used Esther mightily to advance His kingdom, and I believe He longs to do the same with Christian singles. I'd like to share the stories of two outstanding single Christian women, one from each coast. They've surmounted the obstacle that hinders so many and are living fruitful lives.

Dianna Keller, Radio Producer at Focus on the Family

I began praying, even before I finished writing *The Friendships of Women* that God would give me an opportunity to share what He'd taught me concerning that subject on Focus on the Family, the program that reaches millions of women. I had dear friends who (without my prompting!) sent the book in and asked them to consider it.

The first phone call I received was from Dianna Keller. She gently asked me some questions, and I suspected I was being considered, but I tried to keep my feet on the ground and answer sanely. Dianna told me that along with two other producers, a large part of her job is seeking prospective guests, interviewing them, listening to their tapes, and, more often than not, writing them a diplomatic letter telling them they won't be on the program. I was one of the fortunate ones, and enthusiasm won over poise when Dianna called with the good news. She laughed graciously at my response, and we began months of exchanging phone calls and letters in preparation for the interview. She was responsible for preparing me and also giving Dr. Dobson notes to help him plan for the interview. As Dianna and I worked together, I was impressed with her wisdom. I began to visualize her as a godly matron, with years of experience behind her. I was so surprised when a striking, petite, and young woman came down the steps to meet me at the Pomona, California headquarters and introduced herself as Dianna. She was still in her twenties! (Dianna says the usual response people have when they meet her is: "I thought you'd be older—and taller!")

I was intrigued that God would put one so young in such an influential position, and so I asked Dianna for an interview, an interview that produced gems of wisdom!

Dianna told me that even in college she was plotting to avoid a mid-life crisis! "I didn't want to end up," she said, "like King Solomon in Ecclesiastes, saying, 'Meaningless, meaningless, my life is meaningless.'"

In college, Dianna enjoyed dating many different men but did not meet a special man who would become her loving husband. Near the end of her college education, Dianna had a winter term in Rome. With emotion in her voice, Dianna said:

> As I visited the sites of the early church, I appreciated in a new way what is meant by the "community of the saints"—that band of Christians in every century who have remained faithful to God. And I realized that despite the evil in this world, God continues to build His church and it will prevail to the end of time.

That experience showed Dianna that she was serving a God who is holy and sovereign. When she graduated from college there was no husband to stand beside her, but she believed God would be with her. And the same God who orchestrated the events in Esther's life, as she stepped out in faith, worked

in Dianna's life as she called *Focus* and asked if they had any
openings. "They did," Dianna said, "and something resonated
that this was the right direction to go." Interviews resulted in
a job, and within weeks she'd packed up her bags and moved
from Florida to California. She said:

> It's probably a good thing I didn't have much time to
> think about the decision because I am a lot like Little
> Much Afraid in *Hinds' Feet In High Places*. Before I left
> Florida, I asked everyone I knew to pray for me whenev-
> er they heard the Focus on the Family theme song on
> the radio, and then I jumped in with both feet!

God *was* with Dianna, and she moved up to the position she
holds today as supervising producer. Vulnerably, she told me
about going through a crisis point when she turned thirty last
year.

> I was surprised how hard it suddenly became to be sin-
> gle, thirty, and working in an atmosphere where you are
> continually trying to help people have a strong marriage
> and raise their children in a loving home. I felt saddened
> I didn't have a family of my own, like I'd been cheated
> out of something I was trying to give everyone else. I can
> identify with other single Christian women who are in a
> community where marriage and family are emphasized
> more than they would be in a secular job or outside the
> Christian community.

The emotional turmoil leading up to that birthday motivated Dianna to make positive changes in her life. She took some
advice from Dr. Dobson, who, in speaking to singles, said: "If
you find that you are not having the social environment that
you feel that you need—change churches, change jobs, do
whatever you must do." Dianna did that, and though it was
difficult, searched for a new church until she found one that
had an emotionally healthy single group and a congregation

that incorporated singles into families. Her quality of life improved dramatically. She said:

> For the first time since college I am once again part of a community of friends who look out for each other, who feel free to drop in unexpectedly, and who have helped me to see that the love of God is best expressed through his people. I believe it is emotionally and spiritually dangerous *not* to be connected to a family or a loving community of some kind.
>
> In the past year I've also become more involved with my sister's family. I love being "Auntie Anna" to my nephew Avi and my niece Sara. I think it's very important for single women, especially those who have a strong nurturing instinct, to be involved in families, and to let their needs be known.

Another change Dianna made was to begin volunteering once a week at Children's Hospital of Los Angeles. She spends Thursday evenings in the 3-east nursery, feeding babies their evening bottle and holding the ones who need comforting. It gives her a sense of connectedness to the world outside her Christian community and is a wonderful way for her to be "Mom" to many babies whose parents aren't always able to be there.

Remarking on the studies that indicate Christian single women lack confidence, Dianna said:

> It is so important for the single woman to determine in her own mind that she is fully adult even though she is not a wife and mother. With all my heart I want to encourage her to resist the temptation to withdraw from life but instead remain involved in the lives of other people, carve out a job she really enjoys, travel, and create a home where she can welcome friends and family. She needs to see herself as a valuable and much-loved child of God who has time and gifts to give.

Even though she believes God has blessed her, there are some days when, as she puts it, she "just can't get the victory." It's times like that when she is grateful for friends who allow her to tell it like it is and grieve for the dreams she is holding onto but hasn't seen fulfilled yet. And she tries to remember the words of a friend who wisely told her, "Don't stay angry at God or you won't be able to receive His healing."

In spite of these hard times, Dianna certainly radiates contentment and purpose. "Sometimes," she said, "I look out my office window and am amazed that God put me where I am, to be able to do what I wanted to do when I started out, to help people." In many ways she sees her work at Focus on the Family reflected in Isaiah's words which Jesus read when He began His earthly ministry:

> The Spirit of the Sovereign Lord is on me, because the Lord has anointed me to preach good news to the poor. He has sent me to bind up the brokenhearted, to proclaim freedom for the captives and release for the prisoners, to proclaim the year of the Lord's favor and the day of vengeance of our God, to comfort all who mourn, and provide for those who grieve in Zion — to bestow on them a crown of beauty instead of ashes, the oil of gladness instead of mourning, and a garment of praise instead of a spirit of despair. (Is. 61:1-3a)

Jean Troup, Director of Greentree Shelter in Bethesda, Maryland

I tracked Jean down after I read her survey form. Again, she was a single woman who had a dream of making a difference in this world and had stepped out on faith to do it.

She shared honestly that she went through culture shock when she began working with the homeless.

> The dreams that you and I take for granted as being attainable, like holding down a job, or living in our own

place, or finishing high school don't even occur as possibilities to many homeless people.

Mostly we have young single mothers, women in their late teens and early twenties, and they've lived on the street with their babies amidst high crime and heavy drug traffic.

In contrast, I'm from Indiana—middle America! I lived on Pleasant Plain Avenue in a comfortable, cozy, loving middle-class home. The Lord has definitely converted me from a sheltered lifestyle to getting out and dealing with peoples' hurts and desperate situations from a faith perspective.

I asked Jean to describe a typical day at Greentree. She laughed and reminisced about a *Washington Post* reporter who had come out to discover the answer to that question firsthand.

We usually have about fifty people, and most of those are preschoolers so it's always pretty wild. When Chris, the *Post* reporter, came, one of the staff and I were talking about one of the moms, who was in labor. We were trying to decide whether to call the ambulance or not. Then we walked into my office and sat down. Chris said, "Is it always like this?" My reaction, honestly, was "Like what?" I guess I'm past my culture shock—bedlam seems normal!

Many of the residents are able to get on their feet after being in the shelter. Jean said:

Most of us have someone to turn to in a pinch, but most homeless people don't know anyone in a position to help. So we provide day care while they get job training or look for employment. They are trapped unless someone offers them a hand so that they can step out of their despair.

Sometimes you think someone will make it on the outside, and they don't. Then there are those you are sure will fail — and they make it! That's taught me not to make judgments, but just to persist.

I asked Jean to tell me about a special moment, one of those times when you are sure that your lifestyle of obedience is making a difference. She told me about a Thanksgiving Day.

We stood around in a circle and held hands. One mother said: "My son and I have had to live in really dangerous situations this last year. And I'm just really thankful to be here, safe at Greentree, and alive."

With emotion, Jean said:

A lot of people assume the homeless are just lazy, but there are lots of complicated reasons for being homeless. We have so much we can't comprehend what it's like to be without, to be trapped. Because I have so much, I therefore have a responsibility to give back from that resource.

I'm so fortunate I can go home for the holidays. For lots of people holidays are so difficult, because they don't have a home. But I either physically or emotionally have a place to go and it's comfortable for me. I can go there and be secure, accepted, and rejuvenated. And it's tempting to stay there! But I think the Gospel demonstrates that God wants us to get involved with those in need because God could have just snapped His fingers and saved us, but instead He died on a cross. It always hurts to get involved, but I believe that is what He has called us to do.

There *are* many Christian singles who are making a difference. Some have gone to the mission field. A study of 19 major mission agencies (20,333 missionaries) revealed that 16 percent of those missionaries were unmarried, and 85 percent of those were female.[9]

In speaking to Linda Gustafson, a single missionary home on furlough from Zaire, she said:

> I feel so stretched and satisfied and fulfilled as a single on the mission field. I think part of the reason for my contentment is that I don't have the media to impact me with their false standards.

I've understood Linda's words better since we have decided to adopt a handicapped child. Though the report shows she has many wonderful qualities, I know that many people in our society, including myself, will at least initially be very aware of her handicap. I have become increasingly aware of how strongly I have been impacted by the mass media, with its distorted emphasis on physical beauty. Now, when I flip through a secular woman's magazine or watch television, the lopsided emphasis seems to scream at me. Beauty! Wealth! Power! Over and over and over again. And, because I've been overexposed to this tunnel vision, this vision that misses the whole eternal scheme of things, I'm the one who is handicapped. Like the blind man who told Jesus he saw men, but as "trees walking," I'm in need of Jesus' second touch. My friend Sara told me that this little girl is going to help give me that second touch. "What a good chance," my friend said, her eyes laughing, "for you to grow!"

The media plays a tremendous role in shaping the values and therefore the lifestyles of Americans. What impact do you think it has on Christian women? How much television, for example, do Christian women watch?

Entertainment is the devil's substitute for joy.

Leonard Ravenhill

Are We Living Differently in an Entertainment-crazed World?

10 Our first TV, purchased when I was eight, was a small black and white set which received one static-filled channel. It didn't entice me often from my books or outdoor play. But by the late fifties, TV's tentacles had grown and caught me, along with the rest of America. I remember, for example, the Miss America contests.

Pam and Mary-Lynn and I gathered in one of our homes with a bowl of hot buttered popcorn and high school wit for this not-to-be-missed event. As we watched the contestants parade their bodies and sometimes questionable talent, we tried to top one another's catty remarks, giggling the night away. It was all lighthearted until the moment Bert Parks placed the crown on the winner's head and she swept gently down the platform, eyes glistening with tears, one arm clutching roses, the other waving and blowing kisses to an adoring crowd. Suddenly the bantering stopped. The room was silent except for those hauntingly familiar lyrics: "Here she comes, Miss America. Here she comes, your ideal . . . " And in that moment, she became our ideal. The adulation of the crowd, the euphoria of the winner, the mesmerizing melody—all this drummed into our impressionable hearts that to be beautiful is to be loved. And silently we grieved because we knew that ideal—that Barbie doll figure, that flawless complexion, that perfect smile—was unreachable. (Dr. Dobson jests that during this moment, one woman weeps for joy and millions of women weep in despair.)

Our world hasn't changed its values since the time of ancient Persia, for the Miss America contest is simply a sophisticated version of the Miss Persia contest. The difference is that the decadent values of the Miss Persia contest were confined to the palace walls. Today, in prime-time America, these values are broadcast continually to impressionable young girls; not just in the Miss America contest, but in nearly every show, every commercial. No wonder my wish under the Wishing Tree was always for physical beauty. Youth, physical beauty, and money are America's gods.

In *Amusing Ourselves to Death*, Neil Postman says that because of television we will no longer elect a homely but gifted President such as Abraham Lincoln. He says:

> As I write, the President of the United States [Ronald Reagan] is a former Hollywood movie actor. . . . Cosmetics has replaced ideology as the field of expertise over which a politician must have competent control.[1]

Everyone is influenced by the values of the media, but women, researchers tell us, are a special target.

Gaining Control over Weak-willed Women

Scripture tells us that in the last days there will be people who have twisted values, including being "lovers of themselves, lovers of money . . . lovers of pleasure rather than lovers of God," who will "worm their way into homes and gain control over weak-willed women" (2 Tim. 3:1-7). Isn't that an interesting passage in light of the modern phenomenon of television? The values described in this passage are the values of television. Author Maureen Rank said to me, "And teachers like Phil Donahue are worming their way into women's living rooms every day and gaining control over their minds."

Producers do everything they can to entice women to the tube, and they are succeeding. Our hours spent watching television are exceeded only by preschoolers. Women, whether they work outside the home or not, watch between four to five hours daily.[2] (Women in general watch approximately four hours of television daily in July and five hours daily in February. They watch less on weekdays.) Thirty-five percent of homes are "total television households," meaning the set is turned on all afternoon, at dinnertime, and all evening.[3]

Most women have a tremendous battle with self-esteem. When Alice Lawhead interviewed Christian women for her book, *The Lie of the Good Life*, she found many unhappy women. One woman, whom she called Denise, said:

> I feel a lot of pressure to look good, to look a certain way. . . . Having fat thighs—I'm always worried about that. . . . Boy, I feel like I should have matured beyond the point where my looks matter so much, but for some reason I haven't. . . . I'd like to be like Hope in "thirtysomething." They show her in her underwear, and it's like she's got no thighs.[4]

Television not only exalts the transitory and is blind to the eternal, but it saturates us with a flow of lies concerning how to be fulfilled. One Washington woman wrote:

> I was influenced by the soaps, by talk shows, by the lie that says that divorce can have minimal consequences. At the time I thought if there was going to be any hope for me, I had to get out of my marriage. I sowed to the wind and reaped the whirlwind: I live daily with the regret of destroying our children and leaving a good man. Out of my brokenness, I came to Christ. And though I'm eternally grateful for that, I still cannot escape the consequences of my sinful act. My ex-husband and I have both remarried. Humpty Dumpty cannot be put back together again.

And a woman from Wisconsin wrote:

Phil Donahue demeans the homemaker, saying things like: "Some women aren't content staying home with a baby at each nipple!" And though Oprah Winfrey is a lot more palatable, she lacks discernment, supporting New Age advocates, the pro-choice movement, and other worldly philosophies. It's hard to watch that day in and day out and not be impacted at least a little.

There are exceptions, but basically, it seems whatever God values, television undermines. In *Children at Risk*, James Dobson and Gary Bauer quote the Rothman-Lichter survey of Hollywood attitudes. Of the entertainment elite surveyed in Hollywood, only 33 percent thought adultery was wrong, 5 percent thought homosexuality was wrong, 91 percent favored abortion, and 90 percent "seldom or never attended religious services."[5]

Radio broadcaster David Mains took a passage which is usually applied to cult members who go door-to-door and quadrupled its impact by applying it to television. Here is the passage:

> Many deceivers, who do not acknowledge Jesus Christ as coming in the flesh, have gone out into the world. Any such person is the deceiver and the antichrist. Watch out that you do not lose what you have worked for, but that you may be rewarded fully. . . . If anyone comes to you and does not bring this teaching, do not take him into your house or welcome him. Anyone who welcomes him shares in his wicked work (2 John 7-8; 10-11).

Like a prophet of God, Mains sounds the alarm:

> Always there have been voices speaking out for what is contrary to the desires of God — it's just that in our day, through mass media, the voices have so greatly proliferated . . . Living in a media-crazy world means Christians must . . . say no to garbage, even when it comes

wrapped in a pretty package . . . If this was true in John's day, how much more it is so in ours.[6]

Are Christian Women Saying No to Garbage?

Surveying the television habits of the women at my retreats was the trickiest part of my research. At first I simply asked them to estimate their daily watching time. Like the readers of *Christianity Today*, they estimated "about an hour."

But I was suspicious. The modest estimate reminded me of an experience with the women in Kearney's Sonrise Bible Studies. The other administrators and I gave them a challenge: "During Lent, give up television." Only 10 out of 150 women took the challenge, because they defended, "Television isn't a problem in our lives." I wondered if they might be deceiving themselves.

I thought it would be illuminating to have the women at my retreats keep television diaries and turn them in, but that was not easily accomplished. I tried placing random television diaries amidst my other retreat surveys with a stamped envelope, asking women to record what they'd watched for a week, and then mail it to me. Less that 2 percent cooperated.

Finally, I found a plan that worked better. I asked the women to consider picking up a "home survey" from me. I told them I couldn't tell them what it was about, but if they took one, they were giving me their word they'd complete it and mail it in. Their forms were anonymous, to reduce the temptation to be dishonest in their reporting. I did promise them a copy of this book, however, if they sent me a postcard with their address.

I need to tell you that my sampling is small, and may therefore present a rosier picture than reality. Yet I found the results interesting, for these women were watching more than the hour estimated by the women at large at my retreats. They watched an average of slightly under two hours a day, which is considerably less than the four to five hours secular women watch, but still a lot of television. The following chart gives a more comprehensive picture:

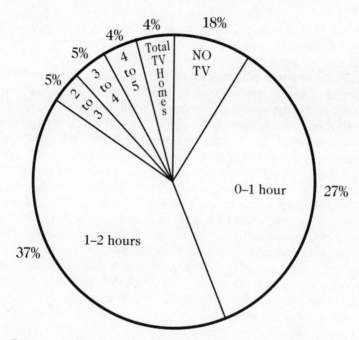

Based on my surveys, one dramatic way Christian homes differ from secular homes is that there are far fewer "Total Television Households:" 4 percent compared to 35 percent. I don't know how many secular women go without television, but I doubt that it is as high as 18 percent.

These two factors lowered the average for Christian women; however, in reality, many Christian women watch nearly as much television as secular women. *How about content,* I wondered. *Is that different?* One way I was able to measure this was by asking:

Do you subscribe to any of these paid movie channels: (HBO, Cinemax, The Movie Channel)? _____

In the general population, 40 percent of homes have one of these movie channels. These channels have a high proportion of PG-13 and R-rated movies. If we are to be obedient to the warnings in 2 John, it seems to me we shouldn't be subscribing to these channels. Most of the women at my retreats seemed to agree, for only 9 percent subscribed.

The women who limited their time with television were also most apt to control content. The more they watched, the more likely shows like "Roseanne," and "Twin Peaks," appeared on their diaries. This supports the theory which Marie Winn espouses in *The Plug-In Drug.* She says that we are so wrapped up in screening our children's content that we miss the vital point that the sheer amount of time they spend watching television robs them of their childhood: of the outdoors, of artwork, of music, of books, of imagination. Children who have strong limits on television time are apt to be the same children who watch higher quality programs.[7] And if that is true for children, it seems it would be true for women as well. I've found that by limiting myself to an hour maximum of television a day, I don't feel guilty when I do watch, I make better programming choices, and I am freed to do the things which rejuvenate my mind and body.

Entertainment Versus Recreation

It's been extremely helpful to me to understand the difference between entertainment and recreation. Entertainment seeks, according to Webster, "to pass the time pleasantly." Most television programs, books, and magazines seek to entertain—and as long as they don't violate God's standards, there's a place for this. But if we don't hold it in moderation, it robs us of recreation, which has the much higher purpose of re-creating our spirits, minds, and bodies. Experts tell us we have three hours of leisure time a day. Since, as Christians, we've been called to redeem the time, shouldn't we spend at least two of those hours in activities which will rejuvenate us such as good books, Christian radio, games by the fire, walks with a friend? In *Unplugging the Plug-In Drug,* a Denver woman writes of discovering recreation after their television caught on fire. Though they went through withdrawal, she eventually became evangelistic about their new lifestyle:

> The difference this has made in our lives is enormous! We had a wonderful winter, full of new discoveries of hidden talents and interests. I learned to needlepoint and my daughter learned macrame. . . . We've done a lot of reading aloud in front of the fireplace. We have much longer dinners now since nobody is hurrying to watch TV programs, and sometimes we eat by candlelight — the kids love it![8]

Many Christian women were challenged in their premarital counseling to go without television for the first year. Several women wrote, that, in accepting this challenge, they'd discovered the joy of recreation. A twenty-three-year-old wife from Nebraska, who does not yet have children, wrote:

> We began our marriage without a television and now have decided not to buy one because we've so enjoyed our time together! We play games, talk, and pursue our hobbies together, specifically, weaving and refinishing furniture. Our free time is too precious for TV.

And a thirty-year-old mother of two also from Nebraska wrote:

> When we were first married, we agreed to not have a TV for a year. Nine years later we have no idea what we'd do with one! We read, play, and work more. We're more content with our lifestyle. My husband used to talk about getting a new car every Sunday and really had an urge to buy. We realized finally that this came after we watched sports on TV at his parents' house on Sunday afternoons. The TV ads work! They make you want things!

Over and over, women who had opted to live without television, told me how their kids had profited because of it. There was less fighting, more reading, more creativity, more outdoor play. Cora Lee, a personal friend who's never had a TV, told me:

> I often get asked how we taught our kids to play so creatively. They stand out, apparently, from kids who don't know how to amuse themselves.

The decision to live without TV wasn't confined to families. A single thirty-seven-year-old from Minnesota wrote:

> I greatly appreciate my quiet, peaceful atmosphere and I feel I more readily reach out to God by living without a TV.

However, only 18 percent of us are living without television. (And that is probably higher than Christians at large, for my retreat women represent a more committed segment.) The other 82 percent of us need to learn how to master the beast whom we have invited to share our home.

Mastering the Beast

Women who recognized they had a problem with television wrote that they had to take drastic measures to gain victory. A Colorado mother of three sons, told this amusing story:

> When I was in labor with Matthew, we checked into the hospital at about 1:45. I wanted to hurry in through the questions at the admissions desk, not because I was in labor or because my baby might be in distress, but because I wanted them to put me in a room with a TV because "Days of Our Lives" was going to begin in fifteen minutes. But they put me on a rollaway bed cart in the hall—until I pleaded with them to put me in with the TV and turn it on.
>
> Then at 2:45, they took me into the room to prep me for the birth. The doctor came in and asked me what he could do for me, and I asked him to turn on the TV. It

was Friday—and everything always happens in the last ten minutes on Friday.

Eventually I felt convicted by my addiction. I tried to cut down, but I couldn't. I had to go cold turkey. I replaced the time spent on the Soaps with Christian reading. It wasn't easy at first, but gradually I missed them less and found my thought life began to change. Now I find Soaps boring.

Many of the women at my retreats said they felt they controlled their time with television but felt guilty that they were allowing their children to watch so much. One woman wrote: "I said I'd never use it as a baby-sitter, but to be honest, I do exactly that."

Some of the ways women had found a measure of success included: unplugging the set during the week, or during the summer; handing out coupons for five hours of watching a week; going through the TV guide and making choices at the beginning of each week; and buying a lock. The women who had the greatest success seemed to be those who had taught their children the value of recreation, often by giving up television for a period of time. I heard many stories, but the one that touched me most deeply was my friend Jill's story: Jill and Russ Wolford and their four children gave up television six months before Russ was killed.

Jill, a pretty brunette, as feminine as her husky husband was masculine, had lunch with me. As we lingered over coffee in a rich oak booth, Jill stroked the smooth wood with her hand and reminisced.

In January of the year their Dad was to die, the Wolford children: Gina (10), Glen (9), Gail (7), and Geri (5) came home from school chattering about a *Weekly Reader* story of children who'd been paid by their parents to give up television. When they arrived, Gina asked: "Mom and Dad—would you do that?"

Russ and Jill laughed, exchanging knowing glances. Russ said: "Oh you kids, you couldn't give up television!"

"Yes we could!" they insisted in unison.

Russ and Jill had been talking about the possibility of taking the children to Disneyland, dreaming of the family vacation they'd never had. So, Russ challenged them: "Give up television for one whole year, and then, at the end of that year, we'll take you to Disneyland."

The children grew wide-eyed. Russ paused and cautioned them:

> This isn't a decision to be taken lightly, so pray about it, think about it hard! Once you make the commitment, there's no turning back, no starting over. We'll have your word—and the television will be off for a year.

The children pondered the challenge for a whole month, but on the first of March, the television was unplugged. For the first few weeks it remained in the living room, staring at them. The kids pleaded to have it removed. It went to the basement and was covered with a big brown garbage bag. A small set in the kitchen was handled the same way.

"The first change we noticed," Jill told me, "was how it affected the tone in our home. Before there was always this intruding blare. Now there was a sense of peace." Jill continued, pensively:

> Russ and I began to realize how much we'd used the set as a baby-sitting tool. We'd forgotten how to be creative. But we began remembering those old parlor games: telephone, dominoes, statues. I can still picture Russ wrestling on the floor with the kids—or lying on his back propping Geri on top of one big foot, swinging her like an airplane while she giggled hysterically. As the weather warmed, we did a lot more outdoor things—bike rides, picnics. . . . And we began to reach out more to people. We talked more—Russ and I had always talked, but we talked more with the kids, sharing dreams, goals, the desires of our hearts.

At the end of that summer, on August 27th, Russ and his brother and a hired hand were moving irrigation pipe. As the pickup pulled up to the last pipe, Russ leapt out, calling, "I'll get it!" A muscular man, he lifted the pipe high where it touched a live electrical wire. Russ was gone in a moment.

Jill said, "I'm convinced that God, in His kindness, wanted us to have that precious time together as a family before He took Russ home."

Knowing kids, I questioned how much time had passed before they asked about Disneyland. Jill smiled and nodded:

> They asked within that first week: "Does this mean we aren't going to Disneyland?"
>
> My intial reaction was, "How can I possibly carry that promise out—without Russ?"
>
> But at that moment, Grampa Wolford was standing right there. He saw the uncertainty that crossed my face, and immediately reassured the children: "Don't worry. You'll be going to Disneyland, just as your dad promised."

During the next few weeks, memorial checks from friends and family came in—fifteen, twenty, thirty dollars, earmarked for "the Disneyland trip." They totaled over $800.

And that next year, Jill and the children, Russ' parents, sister, and brother-in-law all went to Disneyland. "It was therapeutic for us," Jill told me "fulfilling the promise Russ made. It was a very special time."

When they came back to Nebraska, the children asked if they would be watching television. Jill said:

> I wanted to be sure we didn't fall back into old habits. We took the garbage bag off, but left it in the basement. Today they hardly ever watch it. And they always ask permission before they do.

Jill also told me that it's harder, as a single parent, to keep the television off—for she's more in need of a baby-sitter. She recalled an incident one night, six months after the accident:

> I was struggling over taxes, so I suggested the kids go and watch television. When I came downstairs later, I was shocked at the vocabulary coming from the set. I think we'd become desensitized to it when we watched it all the time, but that night I felt like we were being slapped. I asked them to turn it off and get a game out, and they agreed.
>
> It'd be so easy, as a single parent, to go back to old habits. Yet I'm convinced that if I finish the path Russ and I started, this will bear lasting fruit.

I see the dividends of Jill's persistence, for today, three years later, her children are creative, spiritually-sensitive young people. (And for those of you who like happy endings, Jill married a wonderful Christian man in 1991 who is eager to be a good father to the children.)

In the Parable of the Sower, Jesus talked about weeds that can choke fruitfulness out of our lives. Certainly one of those weeds today could be addiction to television. Another, Jesus clearly says, is "the deceitfulness of wealth" (Matt. 13:22).

Often we assume "giving up" things for Christ will lead to a grim, boring life, when, in fact, it is those things that are already keeping us enslaved to a grim, boring life.

Likewise, material things can get in the way of real joy. I've had some Mennonite friends who have helped me with this perspective. My friend, Lorma Wiebe, for example, listened with me to a tape where the speaker claimed that since we are children of the King, we should trust Him to bless us with the best in homes, clothes, and sporting equipment. Lorma turned the tape off and said evenly, "What this man is missing is the beauty of a simple lifestyle. He has no appreciation of what it can mean to be free of cumber."

Do most Christian women appreciate what it can mean to be free of cumber?

*Contemporary culture is plagued by the passion to pos-
sess. . . . Christian simplicity frees us from this modern ma-
nia. It brings sanity to our compulsive extravagance, and
peace to our frantic spirit. It liberates us from what William
Penn called "cumber."*

Richard Foster[1]

Are We Living Simply in an Age of Cumber?

11 The love of money, like the love of entertainment,
is a vine which grows up and slowly strangles fruitfulness from a life. When you read stories of women who've
cut these vines, I hope you'll be inspired!

Terry Westing and her family sold or gave away everything
they owned except for four boxes in order to move to Alaska
to be houseparents for troubled teens. Terri said, "What a
wonderful feeling! It was so freeing to have all our worldly
goods in four boxes!"

Sometimes the joy in the stories I heard bordered on hilar-
ity. My dear friend, Pat Kershaw, told me her delightful story.

Because Pat and her husband had been lifelong missionaries
with International Students Incorporated, they didn't have
the money for an elaborate wedding reception for their daughter Beth. At peace with the choices they'd made for their
lives, they certainly weren't embarrassed to plan a simple cake
and coffee reception in the church foyer. "I did expect, however," Pat said with a grin, "that we'd be able to have cake."
But when they were planning the wedding, Pat and her
daughter had this humorous disagreement:

Beth: "We don't want wedding cake, Mom. I don't even
like cake—and wedding cake is the worst! The

frosting is pure lard!"

Pat: "But Beth, we must serve people something!"

Beth: "How about pie?"

Pat: "Pie! There will be four hundred people. Do you realize how many pies that would take?"

Beth: "I'll bake four. You can bake some. I'll ask my friends to bake some."

Pat: "That's not going to cover four hundred people!"

Beth: "You're always telling me to have faith. I believe God will provide. It'll work, Mom!"

Pat said, "She had me there!" Tentatively, my friend called a few people and said, "Could you bring a pie to the wedding? We're sort of having a potluck reception." The responses were incredible. Pat explained:

Every person I called laughed and seemed really excited about helping. Pretty soon my phone kept ringing with women who asked, "Can't I bring a pie to the wedding too?" They felt left out!

The reception was the talk of the town. When the guests came around the corner from the sanctuary, instead of the expected wedding cake, there was a lovely flower arrangement surrounded by an assortment of the most scrumptious pies you'd ever seen. People had gone all out to make their wedding pie: meringue, ice cream, pecan, and all kinds of fresh fruit pies because it was July. People said, "How can we choose? They're so fantastic!"

We said, "There's plenty—you don't have to have just one!" And still, we took home twelve uncut pies, not unlike the twelve basketfuls of leftovers from the miracle of the loaves and the fishes.

The Joy of Living Differently

The wedding pie story shows the joy that we can experience if we're willing to look at material things the way God does and march to His drumbeat. In an age where the world tells us we need bigger incomes and more things, it pleased me, for example, to see contentment expressed on many survey forms:

Nebraska:
I don't want any kitchen utensils that do only one thing: like waffle irons or orange juice squeezing machines. I only want the barest necessities. When I open the cupboard door and view that sparse sanity, I feel really good!

Iowa:
Through the years the Lord has spoken to us about simplifying our lifestyle. We have no credit cards. We have simplified the holidays. Recently the Lord seems to be leading my husband into ministry—of course, at a much lower salary than we would get in business. This I do not fear—in fact, I'm excited about the possibilities.

Kansas:
When people ask me why we live so simply, I can honestly tell them: "It's more fun!"

Again and again, particularly from mothers staying at home to raise their children, I heard pride in making ends meet:

Nebraska:
Although sometimes I'm embarrassed when I compare my things with others, I know we've made the best choice in deciding I should be home with the children. It also gives me a sense of pride to know that I have stretched our dollars to cover all of our needs.

Colorado:
I can make a $10 Pizza Hut pizza for $2 in thirty minutes!

Many forms relayed excitement in seeing God provide:

New Mexico:
We hadn't received a bedspread as a wedding gift and I wanted one. But God impressed on me to give the money I'd saved for it to a Ugandan lady in need. Two days later we received a late wedding gift. Guess what?!

Maryland:
We have four children and my husband was recently diagnosed with MS. I could be afraid, but I'm really not — because God has always provided for us. Sometimes it's been humbling, like having groceries delivered by friends, but I do recognize it as being from the hand of a faithful God.

New Mexico:
We had a garage sale, promising God the money. We only earned $158. We gave it to people who were smuggling Bibles into China. It turned out they needed $158!

Minnesota:
I was afraid to separate from my abusive husband. I knew our two children and I would be in poverty if I left. But the Lord promised me He would provide for us and helped me to overcome my paralyzing fear. We moved to safety and God has kept His word. Three years later He's still miraculously providing for our needs and is my Rock in every new wave of trouble that comes. Alleluia!

Iowa:
When my husband left a good secular job to go to seminary, people told us we couldn't do it financially! But he graduated from seminary totally debt-free, and with a $300 credit at the seminary. Praise the Lord! We saw God provide for us in *so* many ways.

Many Christian women are, of course, not living simply, not contented, and not trusting God to provide. But it was encouraging to me to see many that are. It's also encouraging to know that those who attend religious services frequently are the most generous givers of money to charity.

Christ Makes a Difference in Giving

An Independent Sector/Gallup survey shows that the more frequently a person goes to church, the more likely he or she is to give substantially to charity.[2] Here are the averages:

Church attendance	*Avg. % of income contributed*
Never	.8
A few times yearly	1.3
Weekly or nearly weekly	3.8

My surveys revealed that the women at my retreats were even more committed in their giving. They contributed an average of 7 percent of their income to a local church and another 2 percent to other ministries. Some gave as high as 40 percent.

Steve and I moved a great deal in our younger years because of his training, and so we've been active in many churches. A few of these churches have given a large percentage of their funds to ministries that help the lost and the suffering. When we've been in churches like that, a greater chunk of our giving goes to the church. But if the church we are in doesn't yet have that vision, then we feel a responsibility to support such organizations on our own. Larry Burkett has said, "Unless your church is doing everything it can to help with other ministries, you need to give to them personally."[3] We choose organizations prayerfully, making sure they are members of the Evangelical Council For Financial Accountability. (This organization will send you a list of members and will also send you free financial reports for up to three ministries, and more for a small cost.)[4] We also have asked questions of missionaries who have seen these ministries operating firsthand. "Are they using the money wisely? Are they involved in both physical and spiritual needs? Are they bringing glory to Christ?"

Many women wrote of the joy inherent in giving to those in need. One woman from Minnesota wrote:

> We used to sponsor a child, but that has such a high overhead, that now we simply give to a world hunger organization and put pictures of some of the children they help on our bulletin board. We also have pictures of the two missionary couples we help support: in Zaire, and in India. We pray for them as a family and write to them. We support them financially and send little gifts from time to time. It really isn't a financial sacrifice, because there's nothing we could do with that money that would give us more joy.

Intriguingly, research confirms that the poor are often more generous than the rich. Gallup found that those with household incomes of $100,000 or more contributed 2.9 percent of their income, while households having incomes of under $10,000 contributed 5.5 percent.[5] Interesting, isn't it? I believe the poor often know the secret of financial freedom.

Christian Women and Multilevel Sales Companies

There are many in our world, however, who teach that financial freedom is based, not on contentment with less, but on earning more. This seems to me to be the philosophy of several multilevel sales companies. (Multilevel sales companies are those in which a contact person persuades friends to sell makeup, or household products, or lingerie, or a variety of products. Then those friends persuade their friends. . . .) The more people they can persuade to sell the product, the more money they will make—and then, they are told, by some leaders, that they will be financially free.

On one of my survey forms, I asked:

> Have you ever been involved in selling for a multilevel sales company? Yes _____ No _____ If so, was your experience what you hoped? Please comment:

My question opened a floodgate. One-third of the women at my retreats had been involved in multilevel sales and most expressed regret. Here are some examples:

Kansas:
My husband and I were very disappointed. We did it so I could be home with our children, but there were lots of nights we had to hire a sitter and go out. We quit a few years ago, at a financial loss, and still have a basement full of stuff.

Wyoming:
My best friend asked me to work under her and I didn't feel I could refuse. But it became a real source of strife, and now our friendship has ended.

Minnesota:
My director quoted Scripture to support a lucrative lifestyle, but I came to realize the Scriptures were totally out of context.

New Mexico:
My friends began to avoid me because they didn't want to buy things. The groups were too materialistic.

Nebraska:
It wasn't until I saw 8,000 women practically worshiping the founder and her materialistic lifestyle at the national convention that I realized I had to get out.

There were a few women who had positive testimonies, who said that the experience was what they had hoped, and that it had even helped them to grow spiritually. One woman from New Mexico wrote:

In my group God's love and direction were very important. We had noted Christian speakers at our conferences.

Companies, leadership, and motives for becoming involved vary greatly. I believe it is possible to be involved in a multi-level sales company that behaves with integrity and to conduct your business in a way that honors God. However, the fact that I received ten negative testimonies for every positive testimony convinces me that cautions are desperately needed. Having heard Christian financial adviser Larry Burkett give cautions, I wrote to his ministry for input. They responded, saying, that though there was nothing inherently wrong with multilevel sales, I should suggest two particular cautions to women who choose to become involved: first, to guard against a spirit of greed and quick profits; and second, to guard against preying upon other Christians.

One woman, whose close friend had been trying to persuade her to become involved in her multilevel sales company, sent me a promotional tape her friend had given her. "What really disturbs me," she wrote, "is that this company claims to have Christian roots. Just listen to his pitch!" I did and wish to share an excerpt with you:

> What would it mean if you could find a way to become truly financially free? If you had plenty of money, would it mean a shiny new car for you? A recreational vehicle with all the extras? A fishing boat? Would you be able then to go on vacation and purchase whatever you want without having to budget everything? If you had all the money you needed, would it mean a new home, custom-designed for you? Would it mean having someone to care for the grounds or maybe someone to take over houshold duties?[6]

Solomon warns us that those who are "eager to get rich will not go unpunished" (Prov. 28:20), and Paul echoes this by saying, "Some people, eager for money, have wandered from the faith and pierced themselves with many griefs" (1 Tim. 6:10). Again and again women told me how they had seen a sister in Christ's focus change after she became involved in multilevel sales. Here are two representative testimonies.

West:
I am in a discipleship group with four other women. One woman has become involved in multilevel sales, and I've seen her focus change from discipling women for Christ to affect women to sell a product. She is trying to get another of the women involved—and I'm hoping it doesn't happen.

Midwest:
My sister doesn't have time for family or friends anymore—at least not true friends, just sales contacts. She used to have a wonderful ministry reaching high school kids for Christ. But her whole life now is geared around reaching anyone she can for multilevel sales. On her refrigerator is a picture of a Mercedes Benz. Materialistic goals are listed on her mirror. She and her husband have an answering machine on which they have included, "Would you like to join us in the Bahamas next year? Ask us—we'll show you how to get there!" It's so sad. She's lost her vision for her life being a ministry and is now just thinking about materialistic goals and of "financial freedom."

I asked a friend of mine who had been involved if she thought that multilevel sales groups were intentionally preying upon Christian women. Although she was recruited for multilevel sales at the American Festival for Evangelism in Kansas City, she didn't think Christians were consciously targeted by the companies. She said:

It just happens. Many Christian women desire to find some kind of work compatible with mothering. Once they become involved, their natural network of contacts are in their church.

The following testimony, from a woman in Virginia, demonstrates the danger of using the church as a place for business:

> I've been so happy that a friend of mine has been coming to church for the last six months, and growing by leaps and bounds. I guess I feel a little protective of her and don't want anything to offend her. So I was dismayed and angry when she told me that she was being approached by people in our church for multilevel sales: first from a man in her Sunday School class, and then from a woman in her Bible study, representing a different company. She said, "It wouldn't bother me so much if they had welcomed me as a newcomer or shown some interest in me before—but they haven't."

In my opinion, calling your contacts from church or Bible study and asking them to become involved in your business is inappropriate because there's a good chance you will offend them and become a stumbling block in their spiritual growth. That danger is augmented when you have not shown any other interest in them, or, when you are not honest in the way you approach them.

I am sympathetic with a Christian mother's desire to supplement the family income and yet not have a regular nine to five job. Yet I believe that our motivation for choosing any kind of employment should be to glorify God. If we seek employment in order to get rich, we are, Solomon says, wading into dangerous waters. Jesus said that the pagans run after food and clothing, but that we should be driven instead to glorify God. If we do this, Jesus assures us, God will take care of our needs. Jesus exhorts: "Seek first His kingdom and His righteousness, and all these things will be given to you as well" (Matt. 6:33).

The only people that can follow this unusual and seemingly risky advice are people who are walking by faith, and not by sight.

Are Christian women today walking by faith?

So we fix our eyes not on what is seen, but on what is unseen.
For what is seen is temporary, but what is unseen is eter-
nal. . . . We live by faith, not by sight.

2 Corinthians 4:18 and 5:17

Are We Living by Faith?

12 It's much easier to measure tangible lifestyle areas such as money, sex, and ministry than to move into the unseen world and discern if Christian women today are living by faith.

I sensed that many of the women at my retreats vascillated, as I do, between walking by sight and walking by faith. Yet stories dotted the survey forms, stories of blessings received from times when they had, indeed, walked by faith. Some were dramatic. One woman from Kansas wrote:

> Parking under a Cottonwood tree one windy March morning, I heard an urgent voice: "Don't stop here." I lifted my foot from the brake and moved forward, feeling a bit foolish. Then I heard it again, "Don't stop here." After going a few more feet, I felt free to stop. Then I heard a roaring sound, stepped out of the car, and saw a city power line fall one foot behind the car, spitting out fire. God saved me from electrocution.

And a woman from Ohio wrote:

> I'd been working on a friendship with my neighbor for about a year, and praying for her salvation. One night I had the strong impression that I should go visit her, but it was past ten, so I was very hesitant. I asked God to help me forget about it if this wasn't of Him, and I found I couldn't stop thinking about her. Finally, at 10:40, I

called and told her that she'd been strongly on my mind, but I wasn't sure why. She said, "Really? I've been reading the Bible and I can't understand it! Would you come over?" I led her to Christ that night.

God urges us to walk by faith, sowing our seed all through the day. He warns: "Whoever watches the wind will not plant; whoever looks at the clouds will not reap" (Ecc. 11:4). To me, walking by faith always has an element of risk—but that's one of the things that makes the Christian life so exciting!

Listening to God's Still, Small Voice

Kari Miyano, an American bride living in Japan, wrote me a sweet letter filled with examples like the following:

Just tonight, in the middle of writing this letter, I went to the drugstore to buy a coldpack for my husband, Tomo, since he has a fever. At first I wasn't going to go since almost every store closes before seven, and it was past that. But then the Holy Spirit prompted me to go. I went, and found the drugstore was open until ten! Not only that, the druggist gave me some free samples! On the way home, I looked in the window of my neighbor's bakery. Though I was in a hurry to get back to Tomo, when my eyes met my neighbor's, I felt I should stop in briefly to say hi. God blessed that small step of obedience, for my neighbor offered to give me some free bread because the bakery was closing! . . . My point is that faithfulness to God puts us in the center of His will, right where we want to be!

The strength that I see in Kari's lifestyle is her sensitivity to God's still, small voice.

When our daughter Sally was four, she amazed me as she recounted her morning's Sunday School lesson. Sitting Indian-style on the kitchen counter, twisting her braids, she was pensive. Earnestly, she spoke up: "God speaks to us in a still, small voice." I laid my potato peeler down, stunned that my baby would understand this abstract concept! Perhaps we were raising a spiritual giant!

Then Sally burst my bubble, saying, "That's why I can't hear Him."[1]

Hearing God's still, small voice *isn't* easy—even for big girls. I can't hear when I don't listen, or when I'm so intent on *my* goals that I'm inflexible when God brings an opportunity.

When we were living in Akron, I'd muffled God's quiet voice with my frantic schedule. The irony, of course, is that I would have told you that I was serving Him: I was leading Bible studies, delivering meals to shut-ins, singing in the choir, moving in a tailspin from morning to night.

The Lord tried to get my attention through His Word. I was reading through the Bible and had read 1 Samuel 15 one autumn morning, but I'd missed the message God had for me. I wasn't really listening to God in my quiet times; I was reading a chapter and legalistically checking it off my "To-Do List."

That afternoon my friend, Carole Chiavetta, came to see me. Carole had been a mentor to me, and so I listened carefully when she looked up from her steaming mug of tea and said, intently: "Dee, I read an interesting passage in Scripture this morning, and I felt led to come and tell you about it. It's the story in 1 Samuel 15 of Saul and the Amalekites."

Stunned because I'd read that passage that morning, I sat transfixed as Carole spoke:

> Saul thought He was serving the Lord, but because he had failed to really listen to Him, he ended up working at cross-purposes with Him. God had commanded Saul to go and destroy all the Amalekites and their livestock. Saul decided to kill all the Amalekites *except* the king and the healthy livestock.*

---

*Perhaps if Saul had been obedient, the crisis in Esther would not have happened, for many commentators believe Haman was a descendant of the Amalekites.

> When the prophet Samuel confronted Saul with his disobedience, Saul was honestly confused. He said, "I have obeyed the Lord's command."
>
> Samuel then asks: "Why, then, do I hear cattle mooing and sheep bleating?"

Carol then laughed, delighting in God's humor. She continued, as I listened carefully:

> Saul's excuse was that he had planned to offer those animals as a sacrifice to the Lord. He tried to justify his disobedience by explaining that he was serving the Lord. But he was not. And Samuel makes it clear that Saul has been sabotaging the Lord's plan when he says: "Behold, to obey is better than sacrifice, and to hearken than the fat of rams. For rebellion is as the sin of witchcraft, and stubbornness is as iniquity and idolatry. Because thou hast rejected the word of the Lord, He hath also rejected thee from being king" (1 Sam. 15:22-23, KJV).

Carole finished by saying, "I'm not sure why I'm telling you this, Dee, but I felt compelled to share it with you."

That day was a turning point for me. I knew I needed to slow down and listen to God's still, small voice. I became much more cautious during that next year about making commitments, not wanting to work at cross-purposes with God. I began to recover the kind of sensitivity, the expectancy, that I'd had as a new Christian—both in my times of Scripture reading and prayer and with the people who came across my path. Interestingly, that was the year that God led me into writing. Had I continued on my own course, I think I'd have missed His leading.

Walking by faith includes a responsiveness to an inner voice. A woman from Wisconsin put it like this:

> To me walking by faith means patterning my life after the man in Psalm 1, who meditates on God's Word day

and night and then walks in obedience to that. It would be nice if God whispered His will to me, but the fact is, He already has—in His Word. If I'm lazy, if I'm not journaling what I'm learning in His Word, if I'm not memorizing, I start walking by sight and not by faith.

His Word Is a Light to Our Path

Our hearts are too deceitful to know His will without guidance from His Word. This world will monopolize our thoughts if we are not allowing His Word to transform our minds. Many studies have shown that most Christians do not spend time in God's Word daily. As I've already shared, the women at my retreats showed a higher level of commitment, but even with them, half did not spend time daily in the Word.

However, one interesting characteristic of the women at my retreats was that many of them listened to Christian radio. Seventy-eight percent of the women surveyed at my retreats listened to Christian radio, and most listened daily. Christianity Today Research Institute corroborates my findings with their study of the readers of *Today's Christian Woman.* They found that these women listened to music on Christian radio for ninety minutes a day, and to Christian tapes for another eighty-two minutes a day. While listening to Christian radio falls into the category of being spoon-fed rather than eating God's Word for yourself, it still is a way of getting fed. I'm certainly not suggesting radio as a substitute for quiet times— you cannot become a mature Christian through spoon-feeding—but it explains how many Christian women who do not have daily quiet times are receiving their knowledge of God's Word. The programs they listed were programs with good solid Bible teaching. The most frequently listed program was "Focus on the Family" but other frequently listed programs were "Insight for Living," "Gateway to Joy," "The Minirth-Meier Clinic," "The Chapel of the Air," and "In Touch with Charles Stanley." God's Word, whether it is received directly or spoonfed by a teacher on Christian radio, is guiding Christian women, helping them to walk by faith.

Here are just a few examples of women who've stepped out in faith to obey a principle they'd learned in God's Word:

Virginia:
My life verse is "Whoever loses his life for My sake will find it" (Matt. 10:39), and I continually try to share our home, food, clothing, and money with those the Lord has brought to us in need.

New Mexico:
If you give to God, He'll meet your needs. The times in our past when we thought we were justified in not tithing, we fell behind in our bills. Sometimes we've tithed legalistically and painfully, but as we've matured, it's become a sheer joy to tithe, and delightful to give more. But no matter our heart attitude, God has always faithfully met our needs, as He promises (Mal. 3:10).

Minnesota:
I was in an abusive situation that resulted in a permanent injury to my body. As I daily choose to forgive, as God's Word insists, I have received greater freedom.

Nebraska:
When reading through the Bible one year, I came to Leviticus. I complained to the Lord that I wasn't getting much out of my reading, and that I particularly wasn't looking forward to Leviticus. He impressed on my heart: "This time isn't just for you." Then I began reading in Leviticus about the sacrifices being a sweet aroma to the Lord, and that confirmed that my quiet times minister to Him. Now I rarely fail to have a daily time of worship.

Florida:
I'm married to an unbeliever who has a very rebellious lifestyle. I've prayed for a miracle in our marriage, but so far, I see no change. Yet I believe that the God I love and

serve is faithful. My prayer is inspired by Joseph's per-spective in Genesis 41:52. I am praying: "Lord, make me fruitful in the land of my suffering."

Perhaps the time when faith is most evident is when the lights go out, when we either walk by faith or despair of life. I love Mirella's response to Anne, in the television production of *Anne of Green Gables,* when Anne dramatically says she is in the depths of despair and asks Mirella: "Can't you *imagine* being in the depths of despair?"

Mirella says, sternly: "No, I cannot. To despair is to turn your back on God."

Women Who Trusted God in the Dark

It seems fitting to close this book with three stories of women who trusted God in the dark, who refused to despair when the lights went out. These women, like the heroes in Hebrews 11, "considered God faithful" and demonstrated that "they were longing for a better country—a heavenly one" (Heb. 11:16).* These are women who are living by faith, putting their trust not in the transitory things of this world, but in the unseen eternal things. These are women, who if they believed in the power of "Wishing Trees," would not wish for physical beauty or for riches but that their lives would glorify God. I believe we could say of these women, as the writer of Hebrews says of the heroes in Hebrews 11: "God is not ashamed to be called their God (v. 16)." I tell you their stories with the hope that they will inspire you to live as they do, walking by faith and

---

*It intrigues me that Esther is not mentioned in the Hebrews Hall of Fame. I believe she provides a powerful model for us, as women, of walking by faith during the four shining days in which she prayed and fasted with her friends, waited on God, and then moved boldly. However, is it possible that God does not mention her in Hebrews 11 because, after the crisis, Esther returned to walking by sight and not by faith? The bloodshed in the end of the Book of Esther, the order by Esther to have Haman's ten sons hanged on gallows, speaks to me, not of faith, but of fear.

not by sight, so that God will not be ashamed to be called your God.

Luci Shaw

In her first stirring book of prose, *God in the Dark*, Luci Shaw tells of her husband Harold's illness and death. After Harold's diagnosis of lung cancer, Luci prayed: "Lord, I promise never to give up on You, never to desert the faith." Luci said that that promise, "like a marriage vow that sometimes staples a faltering relationship," held her during seven years in which she battled to trust her God in the dark "while living in His silence, the sense of His absence." She kept her vow, despite the fact that God answered no to her prayer for Harold's healing on earth. She describes a day during Harold's illness when he called his children and grandchildren into the living room, bestowing a blessing upon them. It was Christmas day, 1984:

> One by one, each of us was crying, out of our grief and incredulity, our sense of loss, pain, and fear. Kris lay sobbing on the couch, her feet in H's lap and her head in Marian's lap. It was a good, hard, precious, difficult, close, intense, unifying time. We all felt the pull between faith and reality—having faith for healing, yet not allowing ourselves to be devastated by NO answers from God.[2]

Luci was the first editor to believe in me, and I'll always feel a special debt of gratitude to her. When I wrote *The Friendships of Women*, I sensed God's leading to go with a publisher that had a Sunday School Series, so that the book could be studied in small groups. That meant leaving Harold Shaw Publishers, who had published all eight of my Fisherman Guides and treated me well. For me, it was a wrenching move.

As I planned to meet with editors of Victor Books of Scripture Press in Wheaton the summer of 1986, I was faced with a dilemma. I was traveling back from Ephraim, Wisconsin to

Nebraska, and I would have children with me. I had planned to leave them with a high school friend, but she called me the night before to tell me there'd been a death in the family, and she couldn't see me. I remember asking God, "Could I possibly call on Luci? Could I possibly ask her to help me while I met with her competitor in Wheaton?" Tentatively I called her, telling her I'd be in town and that I was meeting with people at Scripture Press. I don't think I'll ever forget her graciousness — her offer to have me spend the night, to keep the children, to pray with me concerning my meeting. Luci certainly doesn't walk according to the way of this world, but she has her eyes firmly fixed on a better country. She encouraged me, as women often have the power to do, to live with the same faith.

Recently my heart was gladdened when Luci wrote me with a story of God's faithfulness to her, of His leading her to join her life with that of a man who seems perfectly suited to her, John Hoyte. Their wedding invitation did not surprise me. It said, in part:

> We live in a needy world, and the two of us are well provided for. If you should choose, instead of a wedding gift, to make a donation in our names to one of the organizations below, real needs would be met and we would be delighted.

Then they listed two of their favorite charities, Living Bibles International and Amnesty International.

Liz Duckworth

Another faithful woman whom I've watched cling to the eternal is Liz Duckworth, an editor with whom I've worked at Scripture Press. For Liz and her husband, John, years of infertility were followed by three miscarriages. Finally Katherine was born, only to be diagnosed with Trisomy-18, which is always fatal. Yet Liz and John wrote in a letter of their great gratitude for the week they had with her, which they described as "compressing all the joy and sorrow of parenthood into seven days." They also quoted the verse: "Because of the Lord's great love we are not consumed" (Lam. 3:22).

A few months after Katherine's death, Liz flew to Lincoln so that we could make a cassette album of *The Friendships of Women* at Back to the Bible's studios. During our time together, I interviewed her, probing gently into her wound of grief. Frankly, I was skeptical that one so young could be so mature. "Were you in shock when you wrote that letter? Do you still feel as you did? Or are you bitter?"

Liz wept freely, but shook her head insistently:

> I don't blame God. I know He didn't single me out and say, "You really need to grow, so I'm going to give you this experience." I can separate life from God. And though the pain we are experiencing is very real, so is God's love. He has made that love very tangible to us in our sorrow. It *is* because of His mercies that we are not consumed.

When Philip Yancy asked Henry Brandt, "Where is God when it hurts?" Brandt replied the way Liz did: "He is in you, the one hurting, not in it, the thing that hurts."[3] Liz reminds me of Paul's description of the paradox of the Christian life. He says, "We are puzzled, but never in despair," and "We know sorrow, yet our joy is inextinguishable" (2 Cor. 4:8 and 6:10, PH).

God has blessed Liz and John, since I interviewed her, with a healthy set of twins. But I am confident, had He never given them natural children, they still would have trusted Him.

Connie McClatchey

As I am closing this book it is Christmas time. My dear friend, Connie McClatchey, and her daughter, Andrea, have spent a few days with us. Connie had planned to come for just one night, but icy Nebraska roads kept her here for three days. I am delighted for I treasure each day with Connie.

Connie and Merrill have one child: Andrea, an enthusiastic, winsome teenager. Andrea and our daughter, Sally, became the best of friends when Andrea moved to town. Steve and I are thankful for their friendship because Andrea has a strong walk with the Lord. Before the McClatcheys moved to Kansas last summer, Andrea and Sally exchanged friendship rings, vowing to write and nurture their long-distance friendship.

Conceiving Andrea, Connie tells me, was pivotal in her walk of faith.

> Merrill and I had been married for a few years and had decided it was time to begin a family. As time passed and I didn't get pregnant, I began praying in earnest to conceive. In March of 1974, I had to decide whether or not to sign my next year's teaching contract. I went down to our basement, got on my knees, and asked God to show me whether I should sign or not. In the stillness, I heard an inner voice: "If you believe I'm going to answer your prayer, step out in faith."

Connie, in faith, passed up the teaching contract, believing she would become pregnant. However, by the next January, she and Merrill had not conceived. They finally had tests done that revealed pregnancy was an impossibility. Connie said:

> I went home and asked: "Lord, did I imagine Your voice?" Immediately the following passage came to mind:
>
> Which of you, if his son asks for bread, will give him a stone? Or if he asks for a fish, will give him a snake? If you, then, though you are evil, know how to give good gifts to your children, how much more will your Father in heaven give good gifts to those who ask Him! (Matt. 7:9-11)

I see a parallel in this story to the heroes of Hebrews 11. We're told that Abraham was enabled to become a father because he considered God, who had made a promise to him, to be faithful.

I am not saying that God will always give us children, or husbands, or heal us of our diseases — but I am saying that if He whispers a promise to us in His still small voice, then we need to trust that He will bring it to fulfillment in His time. Connie trusted, and by April of that year she was experiencing morning sickness. Though her doctor was skeptical, he agreed to test her for pregnancy. When he walked back in the room with a positive test result, he said: "Well, Mrs. McClatchey, it looks like we've got some kind of a miracle here."

Connie said:

> I went out and sat in my car and wept. It's an over-whelming feeling to realize that God had been mindful of me. That was a pivotal moment in my life, where I personally experienced the power of God. My faith bloomed. I learned that God is still a God of miracles, and that He is very purposeful in all He does.

Connie and I have talked and affirmed C.S. Lewis' theory that God is particularly tender with new Christians, that He is particularly responsive to their prayers when they are just learning to walk by faith much as a parent dotes on a newborn. C.S. Lewis quotes an experienced Christian:

> I have seen many striking answers to prayer and more than one that I thought miraculous. But they usually come at the beginning before conversion, or soon after it. As the Christian life proceeds, they tend to be rarer. The refusals, too, are not only more frequent; they become more unmistakable, more emphatic."[4]

Andrea was the only child God promised the McClatcheys, the only child He gave them, though they asked for others. And their lives, since Andrea, have not been easy. They experienced extreme financial pressure with their farm, and when they got down on their knees and asked God to undertake in their situation in the early summer of 1985, the answer was not what they expected. Five weeks later a tornado swept through the farm, leaving only splinters behind.

In *Disappointment with God,* Philip Yancy writes:

> Saints become saints by somehow hanging on to the stubborn conviction that things are not as they appear, and that the unseen world is as solid and trustworthy as the visible world around them. God deserves trust, even when it looks like the world is caving in.[5]

Steve and I watched Connie and Merrill trust God after the tornado. We watched them trust when, after Merrill had gone back to school for a degree in adaptive P.E., job offers failed to come. During those two years, though they admittedly had doubts, they also persevered because, like the heroes in Hebrews 11, they saw Him who is invisible and considered Him faithful. (A job offer came a few weeks after Andrea, Sally, and another friend, Robyn, prayed and fasted for a day.) Sally said to me, "But I didn't think God would give Andrea's dad a job five hundred miles away!"

Connie tells me that the trials in her life have shown her what is really important. Her life verse is:

> Whom have I in heaven but You? And earth has nothing I desire besides You. My flesh and my heart may fail, but God is the strength of my heart and my portion forever (Ps. 73:25-26).

Connie reminds me of the heroes in Hebrews 11 who didn't receive all they hoped for, yet trusted God. We're told "the world was not worthy of them" (v. 38), but God commended them for their faith, and has something better planned for them in the next life.

Clinging to the eternal in a world obsessed with the transitory is what separates women who are really living the life from those who are not. It has occurred to me that perhaps the reason God allows our looks and our health to deteriorate as we grow older is so that we might realize what really matters, and let go of that which does not.

The more diligent we are in finding ways to spend time with what is of eternal value, the greater the impact Christ will have on our lifestyle. **He will penetrate every area of life, as demonstrated by the testimonies in this book, if we set our hearts on storing up treasures in heaven. And our lifestyle, especially as women, will have a spiraling impact down through the generations: for good, or if we ignore Him, for evil.**

My life has been profoundly impacted by other women who are really living the faith, even women who lived thousands of years ago, like Ruth, Mary, Elizabeth, and, for four remarkable days, Esther. These were flesh and blood women, who struggled as I do against taking the path which threatens to rob their life of meaning. They were victorious, and now they are alive in heaven, watching us; THEREFORE,

> Since we are surrounded by such a great cloud of witnesses, let us throw off everything that hinders and the sin that so easily entangles, and let us run with perseverance the race marked out for us. Let us fix our eyes on Jesus, the author and perfector of our faith, who for the joy set before Him endured the cross, scorning its shame, and sat down at the right hand of the throne of God (Heb. 12:1-2).

In His Unfailing Love,

Dee Brestin

NOTES

CHAPTER 1: The Wishing Tree
[1]"THE AMERICAN MOTHER: A Landmark Survey for the 1990's," *Ladies Home Journal* (May 1990), p. 136.

CHAPTER 2: Are We Staying Sexually Pure before Marriage?
[1]Garrison Keillor, *We Are Still Married* (New York, New York: Viking, 1982), p. 156.

[2]William Pratt of the National Center for Health Statistics, "Racial Gap Shrinks on Premarital Sex," *The Wall Street Journal* (Sept. 11, 1990), p. B1.

[3]"Study Shows Church Kids Are Not Waiting," *Christianity Today* (March 18, 1984), p. 54.

[4]Ibid., p. 54.

[5]Jean Wulf, David Prentice, Donna Hansum, Archie Ferrar and Barnard Spilka of the University of Denver, "Religiosity and Sexual Attitudes and Behavior Among Evangelical Christian Singles," *Review of Religious Research*, Vol. 26, No. 2 (December 1984), p. 122.

[6]"Study Says Sexual Activity Rising for Young Women," *The Wall Street Journal* (January 7, 1991), p. B4.

[7]Michelle Green and Denise Gellene, "Life in the Shadow of the Dolls," *People Weekly* (March 6, 1989), p. 189.

[8]Mare Beauchamp, "Barbie at 30," *Forbes* (Nov. 14, 1988), p. 248.

[9]"Growing Up With Barbie," *Psychology Today* (December 1988), p. 10.

[10]Michelle Green and Denise Gellene, p. 189.

[11]Ibid., p. 189.

[12]Dr. James Dobson, *Hide or Seek*, (Old Tappan, N.J.: Fleming H. Revell, 1974), p. 72.

[13]Brent Miller and Terrence Olsen, "Early Dating," *Christian Parenting Today* (Nov/Dec 1989), p. 69.

[14]David Seamands, *Living With Your Dreams*, (Wheaton, Ill.: Victor Books, 1990), p. 61.

[15]Ibid., p. 66.

[16]Sharon Sheppard, "Teen Sex Survey in the Evangelical Church," *Christian Parenting Today* (Nov/Dec, 1989), p. 70.

CHAPTER 3: How Can Christian Women Resist the Rising Tides?

[1]Mrs. Burton Kingsland, "Good Manners and Good Form," *Ladies Home Journal* (April 1907), p. 54.

[2]Ellen Welty, "How Early To Bed? The New Sexual Timetables," *Mademoiselle* (June 1990), p. 173.

[3]"Life Visits Mrs. Bunny," *Life* (September 1989), p. 104.

[4]Jonathan ben Uzziel, The Targum, (a pre-Christian translation of the Hebrew account) as quoted by Adam Clarke, "Esther," (Nashville: Abingdon, 1824), p. 808.

[5]*The Complete Works of Josephus* (Grand Rapids, Mich.: Kregel Publications, 1960) p. 237.

[6]Frank E. Gaebelein, *The Expositor's Bible Commentary* (Grand Rapids, Mich.: Zondervan, 1988), p. 789.

[7]Pastor John Bronson, speaking at Kearney Evangelical Free Church, Kearney, Neb., June 1986.

[8]*The Complete Works of Josephus*, p. 238.

[9]*People Weekly* (July 17, 1989), Cover.

[10]News Release: Chicago (AP) August 18, 1988.

[11]Frank E. Gaebelein, p. 808.

[12]Merrill Unger, *Unger's Bible Dictionary* (Chicago: Moody Press: 1957), p. 217.

[13]National Center for Health Statistics, *Mademoiselle* (May, 1991), p. 160.

[14]Decision by Judge Jacqueline W. Silbermann in the Palimony Suit Sandra Jennings filed against William McChord Hurt in the Supreme Court of The State of New York, October 3, 1989.

[15]Lura Henze and John Hudson, "Personal and Family Characteristics of Cohabiting and Noncohabiting College Students," *Journal of Marriage and The Family* (November 1974), pp. 722-727.

[16]John Bronson, June 1986.

[17]Dr. John Whitcomb, *Esther: Triumph of God's Sovereignty* (Chicago, Moody Press: 1979), pp. 22-24.

[18]J. Timothy Woodroof, "Reference Groups, Religiousity, and Premarital Sexual Activity," *Journal for the Scientific Study of Religion*, vol. 25 (1986), pp. 436-460.

CHAPTER 4: Are We Committed to Our Marriages?

[1]Jack D. Jernigan and Steven L. Nock, "Religiosity and Family Stability: Do Families That Pray Together Stay Together?" Department of Sociology, University of Virginia, November, 1983, p. 2. (A revision of paper presented at annual meetings of the Society for the Scientific Study of Religion in Knoxville, Tenn., Nov. 6, 1983).

[2]Ibid. et. al., p. 2.

[3]Tr. Balakrishnan, "A Hazard Analysis of Co-Variants of Marriage Disillusion in Canada," *Journal of Demography*, Volume 24 (1987), pp. 398-400.

[4]Jernigan and Nock, p. 19.

[5]Ibid, pp. 12-13.

[6]Dee Brestin, *Finders Keepers* (Wheaton, Ill.: Harold Shaw, 1983), P. 154. (Material revised.)

[7]"THE AMERICAN MOTHER: A Landmark Survey for the 1990s," *Ladies Home Journal* (May 1990).

[8]John Bronson, June 1986.

[9]Marabel Morgan, *The Total Woman* (New York: Pocket Books, 1975), p. 60.

[10]Erica Diamond, "A Fascinating Woman Gets Sprung or If Marabel Could Only See Me Now," *Free Indeed* (December/January 1978/79), p. 11.

[11]David and Sarah Van Wade, *Second Chance* (Plainfield, N.J.: Logos International, 1975)

CHAPTER 5: Are We Keeping Our Marriage Beds Undefiled?

[1]Robert and Amy Levin, "Sexual Pleasure, The Surprising Preferences of 10,000 Women," *Redbook* (September 1975).

[2]Robert Levin, "The Redbook Report on Premarital and Ex-

tramarital Sex," *Redbook* (October 1975), p. 38.

[3]Karen Burton Mains, speaking at The Decision School of Writing at Northwestern College, August 2, 1987.

[4]Dee Brestin, "Letters to the Editor," *Redbook* (December 1975).

CHAPTER 6: Does Our Lifestyle Demonstrate That We Value Our Children?

[1]Interview with Ann Landers, *New Woman* (September 1987), p. 98.

[2]"THE AMERICAN MOTHER": A Landmark Survey for the 1990s," *Ladies Home Journal* (May 1990), p. 136.

[3]"Religion and Fertility in the United States," William Mosher et al. *Journal of Demography* Volume 23 (1983), p. 370-374.

[4]John P. Marcum, "Explaining Protestant Fertility: Belief, Commitment, and Homogamy," *The Sociological Quarterly*, Volume 27, Number 4 (1986), p. 554.

[5]Allan McCutcheon, "Denominations and Religious Intermarriage: Trends Among White Americans in the 20th Century," *Review of Religious Research* (March 1988), p. 218.

[6]Gigi Tchividjian, *Sincerely . . . Gigi*, (Grand Rapids, Mich.: Zondervan, 1984), p. 36.

[7]Holt International Children's Services, P.O. Box 2880, Eugene, Ore. 97402

[8]John P. Marcum, p. 554.

[9]"THE AMERICAN MOTHER"

[10]Ibid.

[11]James Dobson, *Dare to Discipline* (Wheaton, Ill.: Tyndale, 1970)

[12]Larry Christenson, "God's Order for Children," *The Christian Family* (Minneapolis: Dimension Tapes, Bethany Fellowship)

[13]Mary Y. Morgan and John Scanzoni, "Religious Orientations and Women's Expectant Continuity in The Labor Force," *Journal of Marriage and the Family*, Volume 49 (1987), p. 367-379.

[14]"Ministering to Women in the '90s," The Rocky Mountain Conservative Baptist Association, Wheat Ridge, Colo.

[15]Bradley Hertel, "Gender, Religious Identity and Work Force Participation," *Journal for the Scientific Study of Religion,* Volume 24 (4) (1988), p. 553-573.

[16]"The Woman's Work Poll," *Parents Magazine* (July, 1983), p. 66-68.

[17]H. Wayne House, *Schooling Choices* (Portland, Ore.: Multnomah, 1988) p. 201.

[18]For information about associations in your state, contact: Christian Life Workshops, 180 S.E. Kane Road, Gresham, Ore. 97080.

[19]H. Wayne House, p. 187.

CHAPTER 7: Is Our Lifestyle Free of Prejudice?

[1]Frank E. Gaebelein, *The Expositor's Bible Commentary* (Grand Rapids, Mich.: Zondervan, 1988), p. 789.

[2]Pastor John Bronson, June 1986.

[3]Bernard Spilka, Ralph W. Hood, Jr., and Richard L. Gorsuch, *The Psychology of Religion: An Empirical Approach* (Englewood Cliffs, N.J.: Prentice-Hall, 1985), p. 270-272.

[4]"THE AMERICAN MOTHER: A Landmark Survey for the 1990s," *Ladies Home Journal* (May 1990), p. 136.

[5]Vance Packard, *The Status Seekers* (New York: David Mckay Co. Inc., 1959), p. 194.

[6]Ibid, pp. 196-197.

[7]Dee Brestin, *Finders Keepers* (Wheaton, Ill.: Harold Shaw, 1983), pp. 11-13. (Material revised.)

CHAPTER 8: What Is a Woman's Style of Ministry?

[1]Anastasia Toufexis, "Coming From a Different Place," *Time Magazine: Women The Road Ahead* (Fall 1990), p. 64.

[2]Sheldon Vanauken, *A Severe Mercy: Davy's Edition* (San Francisco,: Harper and Row, 1977), p. 51.

[3]Anastasia Toufexis, p. 64..

[4]Deborah Tannen, *You Just Don't Understand: Men and Women in Conversation,* (New York: William Morrow and Company, Inc., 1990.) pp. 62, 77.

[5]Barbara Rudolph, "Why Can't A Woman Manage More

Like . . . a Woman?" *Time Magazine: Women the Road Ahead* (Fall 1990), p. 53.

[6]George Barna, *The Frog in the Kettle* (Ventura, Cal.: Regal Books, 1990), p. 118.

[7]Service for Infertile Couples, Baron von Davis, 1989, Hope Chapel, 6701 Arroyo Seca, Austin, Texas 78757. (A tape of Merry's story can be ordered for $3.00 plus postage.)

[8]Joy Dawson, "Team Ministry," Speaking at a Seattle Leadership Conference, March 1988.

[9]Ibid.

[10]Dee Brestin, *Finders Keepers* (Wheaton, Ill.: Harold Shaw, 1983), pp. 14-16, 20. (Material revised.)

CHAPTER 9: Are We Making a Difference in Our World?

[1]Dee Brestin, *Finders Keepers* (Wheaton, Ill.: Harold Shaw, 1983), p. 174. (Material revised.)

[2]Catherine Johnson, Ph.D., "The New Woman Ethics Report," *New Woman*, (May 1990).

[3]"Religious Faith: Firm Foundation for Charity," *Christianity Today* (November 19, 1990), p. 63.

[4]John Stott, "Why Christians Must Be Involved, *Citizen* (Focus on the Family, May 20, 1991), p. 8.)

[5]Philip Yancey, *Disappointment With God* (Grand Rapids, Mich.: Zondervan, 1988), p. 93.

[6]Moms in Touch International, P.O. Box 1120, Poway, Cal. 92074-1120.

[7]Francis Bacon, "Of Marriage and Single Life," *The Great Thoughts* (New York, N.Y.: Ballantine Books, 1985).

[8]Patricia Ward and Martha Stout, *Christian Women at Work* (Grand Rapids, Mich.: Zondervan, 1981), p. 16.

[9]Howard Erickson, "Single Missionary Survey," *Fundamentalist Journal*, (February 1989), p. 27.

CHAPTER 10: Are We Living Differently in an Entertainment-crazed World?

[1]Neil Postman, *Amusing Ourselves To Death* (New York, N.Y.:

Penguin Books, 1985), p. 4.

[2]Don Schultz, Dennis Marten, and William Brown, *Strategic Ad Campaigns*, (Lincolnwood, Ill., NTC Business Books, 1988), p. 355.

[3]"Time: How We Use It, How We Feel About It" *Family Circle* (November 27, 1990).

[4]Alice Slaikeu Lawhead, *The Lie of The Good Life* (Portland, Ore.: Multnomah Press, 1989), p. 40.

[5]Dr. James Dobson and Gary L. Bauer, *Children at Risk*, (Dallas: Word, 1990), p. 210.

[6]David Mains, "Chapel of the Air," Wheaton, Ill., April 2, 1984.

[7]Marie Winn, *The Plug-In Drug* (New York: Viking, 1985), p. 3.

[8]Marie Winn, *Unplugging the Plug-In Drug* (New York, N.Y.: Penguin Books, 1987), p. 18.

[9]Dee Brestin, *Finders Keepers* (Wheaton, Ill.: Harold Shaw, 1983), p. 53.

CHAPTER 11: Are We Living Simply in an Age of Cumber?

[1]Richard Foster, *Freedom of Simplicity* (San Francisco, Harper and Row, 1981), p. 3.

[2]"Religious Faith: Firm Foundation for Charity," *Christianity Today* (November 19, 1990), p. 63.

[3]Larry Burkett, Radio Broadcast of "Your Money in Changing Times," December 1990.

[4]Evangelical Council for Financial Accountability: P.O. Box 17456, Washington D.C. 20041 (1-800-323-9473).

[5]"Religious Faith: Firm Foundation for Charity"

[6]Ty Boyd, "In Search of Financial Freedom" Network of Business Opportunity Entrepreneurs, Distributed by F.D.C. Inc, Charlotte, N.C. 1986.

CHAPTER 12. Are We Living by Faith?

[1]Dee Brestin, *Finders Keepers* (Wheaton, Ill.: Harold Shaw, 1983), p. 119.

[2]Luci Shaw, *God in the Dark* (Grand Rapids, Mich.: Zondervan, 1989), p. 64.

[3]Philip Yancy, *Disappointment with God* (Grand Rapids, Mich.: Zondervan, 1988), p. 183.

[4]Ibid., p. 208.

[5]Ibid., p. 205.